30-MINUTE MEALS

igloobooks

Published in 2015
by Igloo Books Ltd
Cottage Farm
Sywell
NN6 0BJ
www.igloobooks.com

Food photography and recipe development: PhotoCuisine UK
Front and back cover images © PhotoCuisine UK

LEO002 0115
2 4 6 8 10 9 7 5 3 1
ISBN 978-1-78440-155-9

Printed and manufactured in China

Contents

Breakfasts

Apricot and almond rolls

Preparation time
10 minutes

Cooking time
20 minutes

Makes 6

Ingredients

200 g / 7 oz / 1 ¾ cups
   dried apricots
50 g / 1 ¾ oz / ½ cup
   blanched almonds
50 g / 1 ¾ oz / ½ cup
   ground almonds
4 tbsp apricot jam (jelly)
½ tsp almond extract
500 g / 1 lb 2 oz all-butter
   puff pastry
1 egg, beaten
2 tbsp granulated sugar

Method

1. Preheat the oven to 220°C (200°C fan) / 425F / gas 7.

2. Put the apricots and blanched almonds in a food processor and pulse until finely chopped. Add the ground almonds, jam and almond extract and pulse again until the mixture forms a ball.

3. Roll out the pastry on a lightly floured surface into a large rectangle and cut in half lengthways. Shape the apricot mixture into two long sausages the length of the pastry strips and lay them on top.

4. Fold over the pastry to enclose and seal the edge with beaten egg, pressing down firmly to seal. Cut each roll into three lengths and transfer them to a baking tray.

5. Brush the tops with beaten egg, score the tops and sprinkle with sugar, then bake for 20 minutes or until golden brown and cooked through.

Smart tip

Look out for ready-rolled puff pastry and save even more time.

Mushroom fricassee with eggs

Preparation time
10 minutes

Cooking time
20 minutes

Serves 2

Ingredients

1 tbsp olive oil
2 tbsp butter
150 g / 5 ½ oz / 2 cups button
    mushrooms, halved
2 rashers streaky bacon,
    halved
1 clove of garlic, crushed
100 ml / 3 ½ fl. oz / ½ cup
    double (heavy) cream
2 large eggs
2 tbsp Parmesan,
    finely grated
flat leaf parsley to garnish

Method

1. Preheat the oven to 180°C (160°C fan) / 350F / gas 4.

2. Heat the oil and butter in a sauté pan and fry the mushrooms
   and bacon for 5 minutes, stirring occasionally. Stir in the garlic
   and cook for 1 more minute, then pour in 50 ml / 2 fl. oz /
   ¼ cup water and reduce by half. Stir in the cream and simmer
   for 2 minutes.

3. Scrape the mixture into a baking dish and break in the eggs.
   Transfer the dish to the oven and bake for 10 minutes or until
   the egg whites are just set.

4. Sprinkle over the Parmesan, garnish with parsley and serve
   immediately.

Pumpkin waffles

Preparation time
8 minutes

Cooking time
22 minutes

Serves 4

Ingredients

250 g / 9 oz / 1 ⅔ cups plain (all-purpose) flour
2 tsp baking powder
2 large eggs
300 ml / 10 ½ fl. oz / 1 ¼ cups milk
4 tbsp canned pumpkin purée
2 tbsp melted butter
sunflower oil for oiling the waffle maker
icing (confectioners') sugar to serve

Method

1. Put the oven on a low setting and put an electric waffle maker on to heat.
2. Mix the flour and baking powder in a bowl and make a well in the centre. Break in the eggs and pour in the milk, then use a whisk to gradually incorporate all of the flour from round the outside, followed by the pumpkin purée and melted butter.
3. Spoon some of the batter into the waffle maker and close the lid. Cook according to the manufacturer's instructions or until golden brown.
4. Repeat until all the batter has been used, keeping the finished batches warm in the oven.
5. Dust the waffles liberally with icing sugar before serving.

Smart tip
Using baking powder
is much speedier
than traditional
yeasted batters.

Smart tip

Don't add too much salt to the eggs as the smoked salmon is quite salty.

Scrambled egg with smoked salmon and dill

Preparation time
10 minutes

Cooking time
5 minutes

Serves 2

Ingredients

2 slices sourdough bread
2 tbsp butter
4 slices smoked salmon
4 large eggs, beaten
2 tbsp double (heavy) cream
1 tbsp dill, chopped
salt and freshly ground
    black pepper

Method

1. Toast the sourdough slices then spread them with half of the butter and top with half of the smoked salmon. Chop the rest of the salmon into small pieces.

2. Heat the rest of the butter in a saucepan, then pour in the eggs. Stir over a low heat until they scramble, then stir in the cream, dill and the rest of the salmon.

3. Season to taste with salt and pepper, then serve immediately with the smoked salmon toasts.

Pancakes with blueberries and honey

Preparation time
5 minutes

Cooking time
25 minutes

Serves 4

Ingredients

250 g / 9 oz / 1 ⅔ cups plain (all-purpose) flour
2 tsp baking powder
2 large eggs
300 ml / 10 ½ fl. oz / 1 ¼ cups milk
2 tbsp butter
150 g / 5 ½ oz / 1 cup blueberries
4 tbsp runny honey

Method

1. Mix the flour and baking powder in a bowl and make a well in the centre.
2. Break in the eggs and pour in the milk, then use a whisk to gradually incorporate all of the flour from round the outside.
3. Melt the butter in a small frying pan then whisk it into the batter.
4. Put the buttered frying pan back over a low heat. You will need a tablespoon of batter for each pancake and you should be able to cook four pancakes at a time in the frying pan.
5. Spoon the batter into the pan and cook for 2 minutes or until small bubbles start to appear on the surface.
6. Turn the pancakes over with a spatula and cook the other side until golden brown and cooked through.
7. Repeat until all the batter has been used, then stack the pancakes onto plates and top with blueberries and honey.

Smart tip

Keep the pancakes warm in a low oven while you use up the rest of the batter.

Smart tip

Use all-butter croissants
for a rich taste.

Fruit and turkey ham croissants

Preparation time
10 minutes

Serves 4

Ingredients

4 croissants
2 tbsp cream cheese
1 tbsp runny honey
4 slices turkey ham
4 strawberries
8 green seedless grapes
1 tbsp fresh thyme leaves

Method

1. Cut open the croissants without cutting all the way through, then spread the inside with cream cheese and drizzle with honey.

2. Cut the turkey ham into strips, slice the strawberries and halve the grapes, then arrange on top.

3. Sprinkle with thyme leaves and serve.

Coddled eggs with mushrooms and Parmesan

Preparation time
10 minutes

Cooking time
15 minutes

Serves 4

Ingredients

75 g / 2 ½ oz / 1 cup button
   mushrooms, sliced
1 clove of garlic, finely
   chopped
1 tbsp olive oil
150 g / 5 ½ oz / ⅔ cup crème
   fraiche
4 large eggs
2 tbsp Parmesan shavings
1 tbsp flat leaf parsley,
   chopped
freshly ground black pepper

Method

1. Preheat the oven to 180°C (160°C fan) / 350F / gas 4.
2. Fry the mushrooms and garlic in the oil for 5 minutes then stir in the crème fraiche.
3. Divide the mixture between four individual baking dishes and crack an egg into each one.
4. Put the dishes in a roasting tin and add enough boiling water to the tin to come halfway up the side of the dishes.
5. Bake for 15 minutes or until the whites are set but the yolks are still runny.
6. Scatter over the Parmesan shavings and garnish with parsley and black pepper.

Smart tip

Cooking the eggs in a bain-marie stops the outsides from cooking too quickly.

Smart tip

This recipe is a great way of using up leftover mashed potato.

Potato waffles with smoked salmon

Preparation time
5 minutes

Cooking time
25 minutes

Serves 4

Ingredients

450 g / 1 lb / 2 cups cold
    mashed potato
3 tbsp plain (all-purpose)
    flour
1 tsp baking powder
2 large eggs
sunflower oil for oiling the
    waffle maker
8 slices smoked salmon
2 tbsp dill, finely chopped
soured cream to serve

Method

1. Put the oven on a low setting and put an electric waffle maker
   on to heat.
2. Mix the potato with the flour, baking powder and eggs until
   smoothly and evenly combined.
3. Spoon some of the mixture into the waffle maker and close
   the lid. Cook for 4 minutes or according to the manufacturer's
   instructions until golden brown.
4. Repeat until all the mixture has been used, keeping the
   finished batches warm in the oven.
5. Serve the waffles with the smoked salmon, a sprinkle of dill
   and some soured cream on the side.

Poached egg with spinach and bacon

Preparation time
10 minutes

Cooking time
8 minutes

Serves 2

Ingredients

2 rashers streaky bacon
2 tbsp butter
8 sun-dried tomatoes in oil, drained and chopped
100 g / 3 ½ oz / 4 cups baby leaf spinach, washed
salt and freshly ground black pepper
2 eggs
flat leaf parsley to garnish

Method

1. Preheat the grill to its highest setting and bring a wide saucepan of water to a gentle simmer.
2. Grill the bacon for 2 minutes on each side or until crisp and golden brown.
3. Heat the butter in a large saucepan and stir in the sun-dried tomatoes. Add the spinach to the pan, then cover and cook for 2 minutes. Stir well, then cover and cook until wilting.
4. Meanwhile, crack each egg into a cup and pour them smoothly into the water, one at a time. Simmer gently for 3 minutes.
5. Season the spinach with salt and pepper, then divide between two warm bowls.
6. Use a slotted spoon to take the eggs out of the water and blot the underneath on a piece of kitchen paper, before laying them on top of the spinach.
7. Top the eggs with the bacon and garnish with parsley before serving.

Smart tip

Wash the spinach just before cooking - the water droplets will help steam the leaves.

Smart tip

Cut the panettone slices
in half diagonally for
the best presentation.

Panettone French toast

Preparation time
5 minutes

Cooking time
5 minutes

Serves 2

Ingredients

1 large egg
2 tbsp milk
1 tbsp butter
2 thick slices panettone,
    halved
2 tbsp caster (superfine)
    sugar
2 tbsp redcurrant jelly

Method

1. Lightly beat the egg with the milk in a wide, shallow dish and heat the butter in a large frying pan until sizzling.

2. Dip the panettone slices in the egg mixture on both sides until evenly coated, then fry them in the butter for 2 minutes on each side or until golden brown.

3. Sprinkle the French toast with sugar and spoon the redcurrant jelly on top.

Blackberry smoothie

Preparation time
10 minutes

Serves 2

Ingredients

100 g / 3 ½ oz / ⅔ cup
   blackberries
100 g / 3 ½ oz / ½ cup natural
   yoghurt
300 ml / 10 ½ fl. oz / 1 ¼ cups
   apple juice
1 tbsp runny honey
mint leaves to garnish

Method

1. Ensure all of the ingredients are well chilled before making the smoothies.
2. Pick over the blackberries and remove any stalks.
3. Put all of the ingredients in a liquidiser and blend until smooth.
4. Pour into two glasses and serve, garnished with mint leaves.

Smart tip

Blend just before serving to stop the smoothie from separating out.

Smart tip

Cooking the potatoes before grating and forming the rostis helps them to cook evenly in the centre.

Potato and rocket rosti

Preparation time
12 minutes

Cooking time
18 minutes

Serves 4

Ingredients

800 g / 1 lb 12 oz / 4 cups
    waxy potatoes
2 shallots, thinly sliced
a handful of rocket (arugula),
    plus extra to garnish
2 tsp Dijon mustard
1 large egg
salt and freshly ground
    black pepper
3 tbsp butter

Method

1. Prick the potatoes and put them in a non-metallic bowl, then cover with cling film and microwave on high for 5 minutes.

2. Leave the potatoes to cool slightly, then coarsely grate them into a bowl. Reserve a little shallot for the garnish and mix the rest into the potato with the rocket.

3. Whisk the mustard into the egg and season with salt and pepper, then stir it into the potatoes.

4. Heat half of the butter in a large frying pan, then fry flattened tablespoons of the mixture for 3 minutes on each side or until golden brown.

5. Remove from the pan and add more butter before cooking the rest of the rostis. Serve hot, garnished with sliced shallot and rocket.

Full English breakfast

Preparation time
5 minutes

Cooking time
20 minutes

Serves 4

Ingredients

2 tbsp butter
8 hash browns
4 tbsp sunflower oil
4 pork sausages
8 thick slices black pudding
8 rashers smoked streaky
    bacon
2 tomatoes, halved
4 large eggs
400 g / 14 oz / 1 ¾ cups
    canned baked beans
salt and freshly ground
    black pepper
white or brown toast to serve

Method

1. Melt the butter in a large frying pan and fry the hash browns over a low heat for 15 minutes, turning halfway through.

2. Meanwhile, heat half of the oil in a second frying pan and fry the sausages for 10 minutes, turning regularly. Add the black pudding to the pan and cook for a further 5 minutes, turning everything halfway through.

3. While the sausages are cooking, grill the bacon and tomatoes until the bacon is crisp and the tomatoes are hot in the centre. Fry the eggs in the rest of the oil in a separate frying pan and bring the beans to a gentle simmer in a small saucepan.

4. Divide everything between four warm plates and season with salt and pepper. Serve immediately with white or brown toast on the side.

Smart tip

To check if the sausages
are cooked, cut one
open – there should be
no traces of pink.

Smart tip

If the grapefruit is very sharp, sprinkle a little caster (superfine) sugar on top.

Fromage frais with strawberries and grapefruit

Preparation time
10 minutes

Serves 2

Ingredients

6 tbsp fromage frais
6 strawberries
2 tsp runny honey
1 grapefruit

Method

1. Divide the fromage frais between two glasses.
2. Mash the strawberries and honey together with a fork and spoon on top of the fromage frais.
3. Cut the grapefruit in half and use a teaspoon to scoop out the segments, leaving the pith behind. Spoon the grapefruit pieces on top of the strawberries and serve.

Avocado and watercress on granary bread

Preparation time
10 minutes

Serves 2

Ingredients

1 ripe avocado
½ lemon, juiced and zest
   finely grated
a few sprigs of watercress
salt and freshly ground black
   pepper
6 slices granary baguette
1 tbsp rosemary flowers
extra watercress leaves and
   lemon zest to garnish

Method

1. Peel and stone the avocado and put it in a mini food processor with the lemon zest, juice and watercress. Blend until smooth, then season to taste with salt and pepper.

2. Spread the avocado purée onto the baguette slices and garnish with rosemary flowers, individual watercress leaves and a sprinkle of lemon zest.

Smart tip

The lemon juice stops the avocado from going brown, as well as adding a citrusy kick.

Smart tip

Look for fresh soft ricotta, rather than the firm ricotta salata.

Ricotta with plums and walnuts

Preparation time
15 minutes

Serves 2

Ingredients

250 g / 9 oz / 1 ½ cups ricotta
3 tbsp jumbo porridge oats
4 tbsp walnuts, roughly
   chopped
3 ripe plums
3–4 tbsp runny honey

Method

1. Spoon the ricotta into two bowls and top with the oats and walnuts. Stir briefly.

2. Cut the plums into quarters and remove the stones, then arrange on top of the ricotta mixture.

3. Drizzle over the honey to taste and serve immediately.

Cinnamon French toast with raspberries

Preparation time
5 minutes

Cooking time
8 minutes

Serves 4

Ingredients

2 large eggs
75 ml / 2 ½ fl. oz / ⅓ cup
  whole milk
2 tbsp butter
6 slices bread, halved
  diagonally
3 tbsp caster (superfine)
  sugar
1 tsp ground cinnamon
150 g / 5 ½ oz / 1 cup
  raspberries

Method

1. Lightly beat the eggs with the milk in a wide, shallow dish. Heat the butter in a large frying pan until sizzling.

2. Dip the bread slices in the egg mixture on both sides until evenly coated, then fry them in batches for 2 minutes on each side or until golden brown.

3. Mix the sugar with the cinnamon and liberally dust the toast when it's done.

4. Divide between four warm plates and scatter over the raspberries.

Smart tip

Add an extra knob of
butter to the pan before
cooking the second
batch if it starts to
look dry.

Smart tip

Serve hot from the pan or leave to cool before chilling in the fridge.

Pear and blackberry compote

Preparation time
2 minutes

Cooking time
10 minutes

Serves 4

Ingredients

4 pears, peeled and cubed
2 tbsp caster (superfine)
  sugar
1 lemon, juiced
100 g / 3 ½ oz / ⅔ cup
  blackberries

Method

1. Put all of the ingredients in a saucepan with 4 tbsp of cold water.
2. Put a lid on the pan then cook over a gentle heat for 10 minutes, stirring occasionally.
3. Pour into individual glasses to serve.

Nutty granola with coconut

Preparation time
5 minutes

Cooking time
20 minutes

Serves 6

Ingredients

75 ml / 2 ½ fl. oz / ⅓ cup
  maple syrup
75 ml / 2 ½ fl. oz / ⅓ cup
  apple juice
1 tbsp sunflower oil
a pinch of salt
175 g / 6 oz / 1 ¾ cups rolled
  porridge oats
50 g / 1 ¾ oz / ½ cup
  pecan nuts, chopped
75 g / 2 ½ oz / ⅔ cup
  flaked (slivered) almonds
50 g / 1 ¾ oz / ½ cup cashew
  nuts
6 tbsp shredded coconut

Method

1. Preheat the grill to medium-high.

2. Stir the maple syrup, apple juice and oil together in a bowl with a pinch of salt then toss it with the oats and nuts.

3. Spread the mixture out on a large baking tray, then toast it under the grill, stirring every 2 minutes until the mixture is dry and golden brown.

4. Divide the granola between six bowls and sprinkle with shredded coconut.

Smart tip
Using a hot grill rather
than a low oven cuts
down the cooking
time by a third.

Smart tip

Break the eggs into two metal ring moulds in the frying pan for perfectly round fried eggs.

Egg and bacon muffins

Preparation time
5 minutes

Cooking time
5 minutes

Serves 2

Ingredients

2 English breakfast muffins,
    halved horizontally
1 tbsp butter
4 rashers streaky bacon
1 tbsp sunflower oil
2 large eggs

Method

1. Toast the muffin halves and spread them with butter.
2. Cook the bacon under a hot grill until crisp.
3. While the bacon is cooking, heat the oil in a non-stick frying pan and fry the eggs until the whites are set, but the yolks are still a little runny.
4. Fill the muffins with the bacon and eggs and serve immediately.

Quinoa porridge with blackberry compote

Preparation time
5 minutes

Cooking time
10 minutes

Serves 2

Ingredients

175 g / 6 oz / 1 cup express
   quinoa
175 ml / 6 fl. oz / ⅔ cup milk
2 tbsp runny honey
1 tbsp butter

For the compote:
10 blackberries
a handful of blueberries
2 tbsp runny honey
1 tbsp pistachio nuts,
   chopped

Method

1. Put the quinoa, milk, honey and butter in a saucepan. Stir over a medium heat until it starts to simmer, then cook for 3 minutes or until the milk has been absorbed.

2. Put the blackberries, blueberries and honey in a separate pan. Cover and cook gently for 4 minutes or until the berries start to burst.

3. Divide the porridge between two bowls and top with the compote and a sprinkle of pistachios.

Smart tip

Express quinoa has already been par-cooked to save you time.

Smart tip

Frozen berries work just as well as fresh to make the sauce, but defrost before blending.

Pancakes with berry sauce and ice cream

Preparation time
10 minutes

Cooking time
20 minutes

Serves 4

Ingredients

250 g / 9 oz / 1 ⅔ cups plain
  (all-purpose) flour
2 tsp baking powder
2 large eggs
300 ml / 10 ½ fl. oz / 1 ¼ cups
  milk
2 tbsp butter
4 scoops vanilla ice cream
apricot slices, blueberries and
  raspberries to serve
icing (confectioners') sugar
  for dusting

For the sauce:
150 g / 5 ½ oz / 1 cup mixed
  berries
4 tbsp runny honey

Method

1. Put the oven on low. Mix the flour and baking powder in a bowl and make a well in the centre.

2. Break in the eggs and pour in the milk, then use a whisk to gradually incorporate all of the flour from round the outside.

3. Melt the butter in a small frying pan then whisk it into the batter. Put the buttered frying pan back over a low heat. You will need a tablespoon of batter for each pancake and you should be able to cook four pancakes at a time in the frying pan.

4. Spoon the batter into the pan and cook for 2 minutes or until small bubbles start to appear on the surface. Turn the pancakes over with a spatula and cook the other side until golden brown and cooked through. Repeat until all the batter has been used, keeping them warm in the oven.

5. To make the sauce, blend the berries and honey together in a mini food processor, then pass through a sieve to remove the seeds.

6. Stack the pancakes onto plates, top with ice cream and berry sauce and garnish with fruit and icing sugar.

Lunches

Goats' cheese and cherry tomato puffs

Preparation time
15 minutes

Cooking time
15 minutes

Serves 6

Ingredients

700 g / 1 ½ lb all-butter puff
  pastry
1 egg, beaten
12 slices ash-rinded goats'
  cheese
12 cherry tomatoes
1 tbsp fresh thyme leaves
2 tbsp olive oil
salt

Method

1. Preheat the oven to 220°C (200°C fan) / 430F / gas 7.

2. Roll out the pastry on a lightly floured surface and cut it into six rectangles.

3. Brush each rectangle with egg then top with two slices of goats' cheese and two cherry tomatoes.

4. Stir the thyme leaves into the oil and drizzle over the top, then season with a little salt.

5. Bake for 15 minutes or until the pastry is golden brown and cooked through. Serve immediately.

Smart tip
Look out for ready-rolled puff pastry to save time.

Smart tip

Warming the egg mixture in the residual heat of the frying pan helps the quiche to cook quicker.

Bacon and chanterelle quiche

Preparation time
10 minutes

Cooking time
20 minutes

Serves 6

Ingredients

200 g / 7 oz / 1 ⅓ cups
   smoked bacon lardons
150 g / 5 ½ oz / 2 cups
   chanterelle mushrooms,
   cleaned and chopped
2 tbsp olive oil
3 large eggs, beaten
225 ml / 8 fl. oz / ¾ cup
   double (heavy) cream
salt and freshly ground
   black pepper
1 ready-made shortcrust
   pastry case
2 tbsp Gruyère, grated
lamb's lettuce to serve

Method

1. Preheat the oven to 180°C (160°C fan) / 350F / gas 4. Fry the lardons and chanterelles in the oil for 5 minutes or until starting to brown.

2. Whisk the eggs with the double cream until smoothly combined. Take the frying pan off the heat, then stir in the egg mixture and season with salt and pepper.

3. Pour the filling into the pastry case and scatter the cheese on top. Bake for 20 minutes or until just set in the centre.

4. Cut the quiche into wedges and serve with lamb's lettuce.

Tabbouleh with hummus and pitta bread

Preparation time
25 minutes

Serves 4

Ingredients

150 g / 5 ½ oz / ¾ cup bulgar
   wheat
a small bunch of flat leaf
   parsley, finely chopped
150 g / 5 ½ oz / 1 cup red and
   yellow cherry tomatoes,
   halved
2 shallots, finely chopped
1 lemon, juiced
2 tbsp extra virgin olive oil

For the hummus:
400 g / 14 oz / 2 ⅔ cups
   canned chickpeas
   (garbanzo beans), drained
6 tbsp olive oil
1 tbsp tahini paste
1 lemon, juiced
1 clove of garlic, crushed
salt and freshly ground
   black pepper
¼ tsp chilli (chili) flakes
toasted pitta bread wedges
   for dipping

Method

1. Put the bulgar wheat in a bowl and pour over enough boiling water to just cover it. Cover the bowl tightly and leave to soak for 15 minutes.

2. Meanwhile, make the hummus. Put the chickpeas in a food processor with the oil, tahini, lemon juice and garlic. Blend to a smooth purée, then season to taste with salt and pepper.

3. Tip the bulgar wheat into a sieve and run it under the cold tap to cool. Drain well.

4. Stir the parsley, tomatoes and shallots into the bulgur and dress with the lemon juice and olive oil. Taste for seasoning and adjust with salt and black pepper.

5. Spoon the tabbouleh into four bowls. Spoon the hummus into four small glasses and sprinkle with chilli flakes. Serve with wedges of toasted pitta bread.

Smart tip

Blot the cooled bulgar wheat with kitchen paper to remove any excess moisture.

Smart tip

If you have time, soak the wooden skewers in cold water for 20 minutes before using.

Lunchbox ratatouille with chicken skewers

Preparation time
10 minutes

Cooking time
20 minutes

Serves 4

Ingredients

300 g / 10 ½ oz / 2 cups
    chicken breast, cubed
1 red onion, cut into wedges
3 tbsp sweet chilli (chili) sauce
2 tbsp sesame seeds

For the ratatouille:
3 tbsp olive oil
3 cloves of garlic, crushed
1 aubergine (eggplant), diced
1 courgette (zucchini), diced
1 yellow pepper, diced
1 orange pepper, diced
150 ml / 5 ½ oz / ⅔ cup
    vegetable stock
salt and freshly ground
    black pepper
1 tbsp basil leaves, chopped

Method

1. First make the ratatouille. Heat the oil in a sauté pan and fry the garlic for 2 minutes. Add the vegetables and stir-fry for 3 minutes, then pour in the stock.

2. Simmer gently for 5 minutes or until the stock has almost evaporated. Season to taste with salt and pepper and sprinkle with basil.

3. While the vegetables are simmering, preheat the grill to its highest setting.

4. Thread the chicken and onion onto wooden skewers, then brush with chilli sauce and sprinkle with sesame seeds

5. Grill for 8 minutes, turning occasionally, until the chicken is cooked through.

6. Serve hot straight away or leave to cool to room temperature before packing into lunchboxes and chilling in the fridge.

Greek salad

Preparation time
25 minutes

Serves 4

Ingredients

100 g / 3 ½ oz / ⅔ cup feta,
  sliced
2 large tomatoes, sliced
½ cucumber, peeled
  and sliced
100 g / 3 ½ oz / ⅔ cup mixed
  olives in oil, drained
6 spring onions (scallions),
  trimmed and quartered
1 tbsp fresh thyme leaves
a few sprigs of basil
4 tbsp olive oil
salt and freshly ground
  black pepper

Method

1. Combine all of the ingredients and leave to marinate for
   20 minutes.
2. Divide between four plates, season with salt and pepper
   and serve.

Smart tip

Choose the best quality barrel-aged feta you can find.

Smart tip

Store the chicory chilled and in the dark for the best taste and texture.

Chicory, blue cheese and walnut salad

Preparation time
10 minutes

Serves 4

Ingredients

3 heads of chicory (endive)
2 shallots, thinly sliced
100 g / 3 ½ oz / ⅔ cup blue
   cheese, crumbled
50 g / 1 ¾ oz / ½ cup walnuts,
   chopped

For the dressing:
1 tsp Dijon mustard
2 tsp runny honey
2 tbsp white wine vinegar
4 tbsp olive oil
salt and freshly ground
   black pepper

Method

1. Cut the bases off the chicory heads, then separate them into leaves and arrange on a large plate. Scatter over the shallots, blue cheese and walnuts.

2. Put all of the dressing ingredients in a small jar, then screw on the lid and shake hard to emulsify. Season to taste with salt and pepper.

3. Drizzle half of the dressing over the salad and pour the rest into a bowl to serve alongside.

Asian prawn and chicken patties

Preparation time
20 minutes

Cooking time
8 minutes

Serves 4

Ingredients

200 g / 7 oz / 1 ⅓ cups raw
  prawns, peeled
200 g / 7 oz / 1 ⅓ cups
  chicken breast, cubed
2 tsp Thai red curry paste
1 tsp caster (superfine) sugar
2 tsp fish sauce
2 tbsp fresh coriander
  (cilantro), chopped
2 tbsp sunflower oil
little gem lettuce leaves and
  coriander (cilantro) sprigs
  to serve

For the dressing:
2 tbsp runny honey
1 tbsp fish sauce
1 lime, juiced
1 clove of garlic, crushed
1 red chilli (chili), finely
  chopped
5 cm (2 in) cucumber, finely
  chopped
1 tbsp salted peanuts,
  chopped

Method

1. Put the prawns and chicken in a food processor with the curry paste, sugar, fish sauce and coriander. Pulse until the mixture forms a ball, then divide into 12 small patties. Transfer to the freezer to firm up for 10 minutes.

2. Meanwhile, stir all of the dressing ingredients together and set aside.

3. Heat the oil in a large frying pan, then fry the patties for 4 minutes on each side or until golden brown and cooked through.

4. Serve with little gem leaves and sprigs of coriander, with the dressing spooned over.

Smart tip

Don't try to move the patties until they've cooked for at least 3 minutes or they may crumble.

Smart tip

Serve the rolls immediately to prevent the avocado going black.

Mixed filled rolls

Preparation time
15 minutes

Makes 4 sets of 3

Ingredients

**For the coppa and
avocado rolls:**
4 finger rolls
2 tbsp butter, softened
12 thick slices coppa
1 avocado, peeled, stoned
and sliced

**For the goats' cheese and
sun-blush tomato rolls:**
4 finger rolls
2 tbsp butter, softened
150 g / 5 ½ oz / ⅔ cup soft
goats' cheese
75 g / 2 ½ oz / ⅓ cup
sun-blush tomatoes,
chopped
a large handful of rocket
(arugula)

**For the cucumber and chilli
jam rolls:**
4 finger rolls
6 tbsp chilli (chili) jam (jelly)
3 tbsp toasted flaked
(slivered) almonds
¼ cucumber, peeled
and sliced

Method

1. Cut all of the rolls in half horizontally without cutting all the
way through one side, then spread the insides with butter.

2. Stuff four of the rolls with coppa and avocado and season with
a little sea salt and black pepper.

3. Mix the goats' cheese with the sun-blush tomatoes and rocket
and fill four more of the rolls.

4. Mix the chilli jam with the flaked almonds and spread the
mixture over the inside of the final rolls. Lay a row of
cucumber slices down the middle before closing.

Bacon, mozzarella and courgette kebabs

Preparation time
15 minutes

Cooking time
8 minutes

Serves 4

Ingredients

2 mozzarella balls, cut into
  16 chunks
8 rashers smoked streaky
  bacon, halved
1 courgette (zucchini),
  thickly sliced
8 large salad onions, trimmed
  and halved
1 tbsp runny honey
1 tbsp grain mustard
1 tbsp lemon juice
rosemary sprigs for
  garnishing

Method

1. Preheat the grill to its highest setting.
2. Wrap each mozzarella chunk in half a rasher of bacon and thread them onto eight skewers with the courgette slices and salad onions.
3. Grill the kebabs for 4 minutes on each side.
4. Stir the honey, mustard and lemon juice together and brush the mixture all over the kebabs. Serve immediately, garnished with rosemary.

Smart tip

Line the grill tray with foil to catch any mozzarella drips.

Goats' cheese and purslane omelette

Preparation time
5 minutes

Cooking time
5 minutes

Serves 1

Ingredients

3 large eggs
50 g / 1 ¾ oz / ¼ cup goats'
    cheese, crumbled
25 g / 1 oz / 1 cup purslane,
    plus extra to garnish
salt and freshly ground
    black pepper
1 tbsp butter
a pinch of paprika

Method

1. Gently beat the eggs then fold in the goats' cheese and purslane. Season with salt and pepper.

2. Heat the butter in a frying pan and pour in the egg mixture. Cook gently until the egg has set around the outside and is only a little runny in the centre.

3. Sprinkle with paprika and garnish with extra purslane, then serve immediately.

Pad Thai

Preparation time
15 minutes

Cooking time
10 minutes

Serves 4

Ingredients

200 g / 7 oz dried pho or pad
Thai rice noodles
3 tbsp vegetable oil
2 large eggs, beaten
2 cloves garlic, finely
chopped
1 tbsp root ginger, julienned
5 spring onions (scallions),
cut into short lengths
200 g / 7 oz / 1 ⅓ cups raw
prawns, peeled, with tails
left intact
2 tbsp oyster sauce
1 tbsp light soy sauce
1 lime, juiced
2 tsp caster (superfine) sugar
3 tbsp salted peanuts,
roughly chopped
lime wedges to garnish

Method

1. Put the rice noodles into a heatproof bowl, cover with boiling water and leave to soften for 15 minutes.

2. Heat half the oil in a large wok, then pour in the egg. Cook for 1 minute or until almost set, then flip it over and cook the other side. Slide it onto a chopping board and cut into ribbons.

3. Add the rest of the oil to the wok and fry the garlic, ginger and spring onions for 30 seconds.

4. Add the prawns and stir fry for 2 minutes or until they just turn opaque.

5. Stir the oyster sauce, soy, lime juice and sugar together and add it to the wok, followed by the drained noodles.

6. Stir-fry for 1 more minute, then stir in the peanuts and serve immediately, garnished with lime wedges.

Smart tip

As soon as the prawns turn opaque, continue with the rest of the recipe as they will toughen if overcooked.

Smart tip

Chinese sausages can be purchased from oriental supermarkets.

Chinese sausage, broccoli and noodle stir-fry

Preparation time
5 minutes

Cooking time
12 minutes

Serves 4

Ingredients

200 g / 7 oz / 1 ⅓ cups dried egg noodles
½ head broccoli, broken into florets
3 tbsp vegetable oil
2 cloves of garlic, thinly sliced
2 Chinese sausages, thickly sliced
1 tbsp light soy sauce
2 tbsp oyster sauce

Method

1. Cook the noodles in boiling, salted water according to the packet instructions or until al dente, then drain well.
2. Meanwhile, blanch the broccoli for 4 minutes then plunge into cold water and drain well.
3. Heat the oil in a large wok and fry the garlic and sausage for 2 minutes.
4. Add the soy sauce, oyster sauce, noodles and broccoli and stir-fry for 2 more minutes, then serve immediately.

Cheesy courgette gratins

Preparation time
5 minutes

Cooking time
25 minutes

Serves 4

Ingredients

4 courgettes (zucchinis),
  halved lengthways
2 tbsp butter
2 tbsp plain (all-purpose)
  flour
600 ml / 1 pint / 2 ½ cups milk
150 g / 5 ½ oz / 1 ½ cups
  Cheddar cheese, grated
salt and freshly ground
  black pepper
25 g / 1 oz / ⅓ cup
  breadcrumbs

Method

1. Preheat the oven to 180°C (160°C fan) / 350F / gas 4.

2. Bake the courgettes in a shallow baking dish for 10 minutes
   while you make the topping.

3. Melt the butter in a medium saucepan then stir in the flour.
   Gradually whisk in the milk a little at a time until it is all
   incorporated.

4. Cook the sauce over a low heat, stirring constantly, until the
   mixture thickens. Beat vigorously to remove any lumps, then
   stir in the cheese and season to taste with salt and pepper.

5. Take the courgettes out of the oven and spoon the sauce on
   top. Sprinkle with breadcrumbs and return to the oven for a
   further 15 minutes or until the courgettes are tender and the
   crumbs are golden.

Smart tip

A skewer should slide
easily into the
courgettes when
they're done.

Smart tip

Look out for pitted olives and just roughly chop before using.

Tagliatelle with tomatoes and olives

Preparation time
5 minutes

Cooking time
12 minutes

Serves 4

Ingredients

400 g / 14 oz / 2 cups dried
tagliatelle
3 tbsp olive oil
4 cloves of garlic, crushed
½ tsp chilli (chili) flakes
200 g / 7 oz / 1 cup canned
chopped tomatoes
75 g / 2 ½ oz / ½ cup
kalamata olives, pitted
and chopped
salt and freshly ground
black pepper
a handful of basil leaves,
chopped

Method

1. Cook the tagliatelle in boiling, salted water according to the packet instructions or until al dente.

2. Meanwhile, heat the oil in a large sauté pan and fry the garlic and chilli flakes for 2 minutes. Stir in the tomatoes and olives and cook until the pasta is ready, stirring occasionally. Season to taste with salt and pepper.

3. Drain the pasta and tip it into the sauté pan. Stir to coat with the sauce, then divide between four warm bowls and garnish with basil.

Rice noodle and green vegetable salad

Preparation time
10 minutes

Cooking time
5 minutes

Serves 4

Ingredients

100 g / 3 ½ oz / ⅔ cup broad beans
4 runner beans, chopped
200 g / 7 oz / 1 ⅓ cups asparagus spears, cut into short lengths
½ red onion, thinly sliced
200 g / 7 oz / 1 ¼ cups fresh rice noodles
1 tbsp caster (superfine) sugar
3 tbsp rice wine vinegar
1 tsp sesame oil
mint leaves and lime wedges to garnish
white pepper

Method

1. Bring a large pan of salted water to the boil. Blanch the broad beans, runner beans and asparagus spears for 5 minutes or until cooked al dente.

2. Drain well then plunge into a large bowl of ice water. Drain again.

3. Toss the vegetables with the onion and noodles.

4. Stir the caster sugar, vinegar and sesame oil together with a big pinch of salt. When the sugar has dissolved, pour it over the salad and toss again.

5. Divide the salad between four bowls and garnish with mint leaves and lime wedges. Season with white pepper and serve immediately.

Smart tip

Plunging the vegetables into ice water stops them cooking and cools them quickly.

Smart tip

Pricking the potatoes stops them from exploding in the microwave.

Jacket potatoes with tomatoes and feta

Preparation time
10 minutes

Cooking time
20 minutes

Serves 4

Ingredients

4 baking potatoes, scrubbed
75 g / 2 ½ oz / ½ cup black olives, pitted and sliced
100 g / 3 ½ oz / ⅔ cup feta, crumbled
150 g / 5 ½ oz / 1 cup cherry tomatoes, quartered
2 spring onions (scallions), chopped
4 tbsp olive oil
freshly ground black pepper

Method

1. Preheat the oven to 220°C (200°C fan) / 430F / gas 7.

2. Prick the potatoes all over, then microwave on high for 5 minutes or until a skewer will slide easily into the centres.

3. Cut the potatoes in half and scoop a little of each one into a bowl. Add the rest of the ingredients and stir well, then pack the mixture on top of the potatoes.

4. Arrange the potatoes in a baking dish and bake for 15 minutes. Season with black pepper and serve immediately.

Ham and dill pickle salad

Preparation time
5 minutes

Serves 1

Ingredients
3 slices ham
2 dill pickles
1 large salad onion
1 tsp mayonnaise
1 tsp runny honey
1 tbsp white wine vinegar
chives to garnish

Method
1. Cut the ham into bite-sized pieces and slice the dill pickles. Remove and discard the green part of the onion, then chop the rest and toss with the ham and pickles.

2. Stir the mayonnaise, honey and vinegar together to form a dressing, then toss with the salad.

3. Serve garnished with chives.

Smart tip

If the dressing is a bit too sharp, add a splash of water.

Smart tip
If you can't find chervil,
use parsley instead.

King prawn, apple and celery salad

Preparation time
5 minutes

Serves 2

Ingredients

1 Granny Smith apple, cored
2 celery sticks, washed
12 king prawns, cooked and
  peeled
2 tbsp mayonnaise
1 tbsp lemon juice
chervil sprigs to garnish

Method

1. Cut the apple and celery into matchsticks and toss with the prawns. Divide between two plates.

2. Stir the mayonnaise and lemon juice together then add just enough cold water to make a dressing.

3. Drizzle the dressing over the salad and garnish with chervil.

Red pepper and sesame noodles

Preparation time
5 minutes

Cooking time
12 minutes

Serves 4

Ingredients

200 g / 7 oz / 1 ⅓ cups dried
   egg noodles
3 tbsp vegetable oil
2 cloves of garlic, crushed
2 spring onions (scallions),
   finely chopped
1 tsp fresh root ginger,
   finely grated
1 red pepper, diced
2 tbsp light soy sauce
1 tsp sesame oil
2 tbsp sesame seeds

Method

1. Cook the noodles in boiling, salted water according to the packet instructions or until al dente, then drain well.
2. Meanwhile, heat the oil in a large wok and fry the garlic, spring onions and ginger for 2 minutes.
3. Add the pepper and soy sauce and stir-fry for 2 more minutes, then cover the wok with a lid and steam for 3 minutes.
4. Add the drained noodles to the wok with the sesame oil and stir-fry for 2 minutes, then divide between four warm bowls and sprinkle with sesame seeds.

Smart tip

Use the green parts of
the spring onions as
well as the white to give
a varied taste.

Smart tip

This dish is delicious
served with home-
made coleslaw.

Chicken goujons with apple and cucumber salad

Preparation time
20 minutes

Cooking time
5 minutes

Serves 4

Ingredients

4 tbsp plain (all-purpose) flour
1 egg, beaten
75 g / 2 ½ oz / ½ cup panko breadcrumbs
4 skinless chicken breasts, cut into strips.
sunflower oil for deep frying
2 tbsp basil leaves, finely chopped

For the salad:
½ cucumber, peeled and sliced
1 apple, peeled, cored and sliced
1 lemon, juiced
salt and freshly ground black pepper
½ tsp chilli (chili) flakes

Method

1. Heat the oil in a deep fat fryer, according to the manufacturer's instructions, to a temperature of 180°C (350F).
2. Put the flour, egg and panko breadcrumbs in three separate bowls.
3. Dip the chicken strips first in the flour, then in the egg, then in the breadcrumbs.
4. Lower the goujons in the fryer basket and cook for 5 minutes or until crisp and golden brown, then transfer to a sieve lined with kitchen paper. Sprinkle with chopped basil.
5. To make the salad, toss the cucumber and apple slices with the lemon juice and season with salt and pepper.
6. Divide the salad between four bowls and sprinkle with chilli flakes, then serve with the chicken goujons.

Spaghetti with courgette and cherry tomatoes

Preparation time
5 minutes

Cooking time
12 minutes

Serves 4

Ingredients

400 g / 14 oz / 2 cups dried
spaghetti
2 courgettes (zucchinis)
150 g / 5 ½ oz / 1 cup cherry
tomatoes, quartered
5 tbsp olive oil
50 g / 1 ¾ oz / ½ cup
Pecorino, grated
salt and freshly ground black
pepper
basil leaves to garnish

Method

1. Cook the spaghetti in boiling, salted water according to the packet instructions or until al dente.
2. Meanwhile, use a julienne tool or culinary knife to cut the courgette into spaghetti-like strips. When the spaghetti is ready, stir the courgette into the pan, then drain well.
3. Toss the spaghetti and courgette with the tomatoes and oil then divide between four warm bowls.
4. Scatter the grated Pecorino over the top, season with salt and pepper and garnish with basil leaves.

Smart tip
The julienne tool
looks like a vegetable
peeler with teeth and
can be purchased in
cook shops.

Smart tip

Don't overcook the squid as it quickly turns rubbery.

Chilli squid skewers with aioli

Preparation time
25 minutes

Cooking time
2 minutes

Serves 4

Ingredients

4 large squid tubes, cut into
   squares
3 tbsp sweet chilli (chili) sauce
½ lime, juiced
a pinch of salt

For the aioli:
1 egg yolk
1 clove of garlic, crushed
1 tbsp lemon juice
½ tsp Dijon mustard
salt and freshly ground
   black pepper
100 ml / 3 ½ fl. oz / ½ cup
   mild olive oil

Method

1. Thread the squid onto eight metal skewers. Mix the chilli sauce with the lime juice and a pinch of salt, then brush the mixture over the squid and leave to marinate for 15 minutes.

2. Meanwhile, whisk the egg yolk, garlic, lemon juice and Dijon mustard together with a pinch of salt and pepper.

3. Slowly incorporate the oil in a thin stream, whisking all the time, until it has all been incorporated and the aioli is thick. Taste and adjust the seasoning with more salt, pepper or lemon juice.

4. Preheat the grill to its highest setting then grill the squid skewers for 1 minute on each side or until the pieces just turn opaque. Serve immediately with the aioli.

Smoked salmon pasta salad

Preparation time
10 minutes

Cooking time
12 minutes

Serves 2

Ingredients

200 g / 7 oz / 1 ½ cups dried
    fusilli
4 slices smoked salmon
50 g / 1 ¾ oz / 1 cup baby
    leaf spinach, sliced
3 medium tomatoes, diced
½ red onion, chopped
4 tbsp olive oil
1 lemon, juiced
salt and freshly ground
    black pepper
2 tbsp basil leaves, shredded

Method

1. Cook the pasta in boiling, salted water according to the packet instructions or until al dente. Drain well, then plunge into iced water to quickly cool it to room temperature. Drain again.

2. Cut the smoked salmon into bite-sized pieces and toss with the pasta, spinach, tomatoes and onion.

3. Whisk the oil with the lemon juice and season generously with salt and pepper. Toss the dressing with the salad and garnish with shredded basil and black pepper.

Smart tip

Eat straight away or pack into lunchboxes and store in the fridge.

Smart tip

Panko crumbs are Japanese dried breadcrumbs with a great crunchy texture.

Crispy fish burgers

Preparation time
15 minutes

Cooking time
5 minutes

Serves 4

Ingredients

sunflower oil for deep-frying
4 tbsp plain (all-purpose) flour
1 egg, beaten
75 g / 2 ½ oz / ½ cup panko breadcrumbs
4 small portions of pollock fillet
4 bread rolls, halved horizontally
4 tbsp tartare sauce
lemon pieces to garnish

Method

1. Heat the oil in a deep fat fryer, according to the manufacturer's instructions, to a temperature of 180°C (350F).
2. Meanwhile, put the flour, egg and panko breadcrumbs in three separate bowls. Dip the fish first in the flour, then in the egg, then in the breadcrumbs.
3. Lower the fish in the fryer basket and cook for 5 minutes or until crisp and golden brown. Line a large bowl with a thick layer of kitchen paper and when the fish is ready, tip the pieces into the bowl to remove any excess oil.
4. Spread the bases of the bread rolls with tartare sauce, then top with the fish and replace the lids. Serve immediately, garnished with lemon pieces.

Smoked salmon and sun-dried tomato pasta

Preparation time
5 minutes

Cooking time
12 minutes

Serves 4

Ingredients

400 g / 14 oz / 3 cups dried
  farfalle
150 g / 5 ½ oz / 1 cup
  smoked salmon, chopped
100 g / 3 ½ oz / ½ cup
  sun-dried tomatoes, plus
  4 tbsp of the oil
75 g / 2 ½ oz / ½ cup
  kalamata olives, pitted
1 lemon, juiced
basil leaves to garnish

Method

1. Cook the pasta in boiling, salted water according to the packet instructions or until al dente.
2. Drain well, then toss with the smoked salmon, sun-dried tomatoes and olives.
3. Whisk the lemon juice with the sun-dried tomato oil and drizzle it over the pasta, then toss again. Serve garnished with basil leaves.

Smart tip
Serve in hot bowls as the cold ingredients will lower the temperature of the pasta.

Smart tip
Cutting the vegetables
into small cubes makes
them cook quickly
and evenly.

Minestrone with gnocchi

Preparation time
5 minutes

Cooking time
20 minutes

Serves 4

Ingredients

2 tbsp olive oil
1 onion, chopped
2 cloves of garlic, finely
chopped
1 carrot, diced
1 celery stick, diced
1 courgette (zucchini), diced
4 medium tomatoes, peeled
and chopped
100 g / 3 ½ oz / ⅔ cup peas,
defrosted if frozen
2 tbsp concentrated tomato
purée
1.2 litres / 2 pints / 4 ¾ cups
vegetable stock
250 g / 9 oz / 1 ½ cups potato
gnocchi
salt and freshly ground
black pepper
basil leaves to garnish

Method

1. Heat the oil in a saucepan and fry the onion and garlic for
5 minutes. Stir in the rest of the vegetables, then add the
tomato purée and stock and bring to the boil.

2. Simmer for 10 minutes, then add the gnocchi and cook for
4 more minutes or until they are all floating.

3. Season to taste with salt and pepper before ladling into warm
bowls and garnishing with basil.

Lamb, clementine and pomegranate salad

Preparation time
5 minutes

Cooking time
6 minutes

Serves 2

Ingredients

6 lamb medallions
2 tbsp olive oil
salt and freshly ground
   black pepper
1 clementine, peeled and
   separated into segments
3 tbsp pomegranate seeds
4 large radicchio leaves,
   sliced
a small bunch of watercress,
   washed and picked

Method

1. Heat a griddle pan until smoking hot. Brush the lamb with oil and season with salt and pepper, then griddle for 3 minutes on each side.

2. Meanwhile, toss the clementine segments with the pomegranate seeds, radicchio and watercress and divide between two bowls.

3. Top with the lamb and serve immediately.

Smart tip

Wrapping the Camembert with foil will stop any leaks if the box breaks.

Baked Camembert

Preparation time
10 minutes

Cooking time
15 minutes

Serves 4

Ingredients

1 Camembert
6 new potatoes, halved
1 head of red chicory
  (endive), separated into
  leaves
3 young celery hearts,
  quartered

Method

1. Preheat the oven to 180°C (160°C fan) / 350F / gas 4 and put a large pan of salted water on to boil.

2. Take the Camembert out of its box and remove the paper. Put it back in the bottom of the box, sit it in a large square of foil, then bring up the sides and scrunch to seal.

3. Bake the Camembert for 15 minutes or until the centre has melted.

4. Meanwhile, boil the potatoes for 12 minutes or until tender, then drain well.

5. Remove the foil and pull back the skin of the Camembert and serve with the potatoes, chicory and celery for dipping.

Salmon and cod fishcakes

Preparation time
20 minutes

Cooking time
8 minutes

Serves 4

Ingredients

4 tbsp plain (all-purpose)
    flour
1 egg, beaten
75 g / 2 ½ oz / ½ cup panko
    breadcrumbs
450 g / 1 lb / 2 cups leftover
    mashed potato
200 g / 7 oz / 1 ¼ cup skinless
    cod fillet, chopped
200 g / 7 oz / 1 ¼ cup skinless
    salmon fillet, chopped
2 tsp Dijon mustard
2 tbsp fresh dill, finely
    chopped
sunflower oil for deep-frying
lettuce and tomatoes
    for serving

Method

1. Put the flour, egg and panko breadcrumbs in three separate bowls.

2. Mix the mashed potato with the cod, salmon, mustard and dill, then shape it into eight patties.

3. Dip the fish cakes alternately in the flour, egg and breadcrumbs and shake off any excess.

4. Heat the oil in a deep fat fryer, according to the manufacturer's instructions, to a temperature of 180°C (350F).

5. Lower the fishcakes in the fryer basket and cook for 8 minutes or until crisp and golden brown. Line a large bowl with a thick layer of kitchen paper and when they are ready, tip them into the bowl to remove any excess oil.

6. Serve with lettuce and tomatoes.

Smart tip
You can also use dried
dill in this recipe, but
reduce the quantity
to ¼ tsp.

Smart tip
Air-dried beef is sold as viande des grisons in Switzerland and bresaola in Italy.

Pea and feta omelette

Preparation time
5 minutes

Cooking time
5 minutes

Serves 1

Ingredients

3 large eggs
2 tbsp frozen peas, defrosted
salt and freshly ground
   black pepper
1 tbsp butter
2 slices air-dried beef,
   chopped
50 g / 1 ¾ oz / ¼ cup feta,
   crumbled
1 tbsp chives, chopped

Method

1. Gently beat the eggs then stir in the peas and season with salt and pepper.
2. Heat the butter in a frying pan and pour in the egg mixture. Cook gently until the egg has set around the outside.
3. Top with the air-dried beef, feta and chives and cook until the centre is just slightly runny.
4. Fold over the omelette and slide it onto a warm plate to serve.

Main
Meals

Rack of lamb with peas and Madeira gravy

Preparation time
8 minutes

Cooking time
20 minutes

Serves 4

Ingredients

2 x 6-bone racks of lamb
2 tbsp olive oil
salt and freshly ground black
  pepper
150 g / 5 ½ oz / 1 cup sugar
  snap peas
150 g / 5 ½ oz / 1 cup fresh
  peas, podded
a few sprigs of fresh coriander
  (cilantro)

For the gravy:
1 large onion, finely chopped
2 tbsp butter
2 tbsp Madeira
a pinch of salt
250 ml / 9 fl. oz / 1 cup
  good-quality lamb stock

Method

1. Preheat the oven to 220°C (200°C fan) / 430F / gas 7 and heat a frying pan until smoking hot.

2. Brush the lamb with oil and sear it all over in the frying pan, then season with salt and pepper and roast in the oven for 10 minutes. Leave the lamb to rest somewhere warm for 5 minutes.

3. Meanwhile, fry the onion in the butter for 10 minutes or until starting to caramelise. Add the Madeira and a pinch of salt and bubble away almost to nothing. Add the stock and simmer gently until reduced and slightly thickened.

4. While the gravy is cooking, boil the sugar snaps and peas for 4 minutes or until al dente.

5. Cut the lamb into individual chops and serve 3 per person on a bed of peas and sugar snaps. Strain the gravy through a sieve to get rid of the onions and spoon it around the plate. Garnish the lamb with coriander.

Smart tip
If you prefer your lamb cooked well-done, roast for 18 minutes instead.

Smart tip

Steaming the cabbage and salmon together saves on washing up.

Salmon with Chinese cabbage and soy

Preparation time
18 minutes

Cooking time
6 minutes

Serves 4

Ingredients

4 tbsp dark soy sauce
1 tbsp sesame oil
1 red chilli (chili), sliced
freshly ground black pepper
4 portions salmon fillet
4 portions microwave rice
½ Chinese cabbage, sliced

Method

1. Mix the soy sauce with the sesame oil, chilli and black pepper. Pour the mixture over the salmon and leave to marinate for 15 minutes.

2. Microwave the rice according to packet instructions.

3. Preheat a steamer. Put the cabbage in the steamer basket and top with the marinated salmon. Steam for 6 minutes or until the salmon is starting to flake round the edges but is still slightly translucent in the centre.

4. Serve immediately with the rice.

Grilled king prawns with spicy giant couscous

Preparation time
5 minutes

Cooking time
25 minutes

Serves 2

Ingredients

4 tbsp olive oil
1 red onion, chopped
2 cloves of garlic, finely
   chopped
1 red pepper, chopped
100 g / 3 ½ oz / ½ cup giant
   couscous
200 ml / 7 fl. oz / ¾ cup
   vegetable stock
1 tsp smoked paprika
10 raw king prawns
1 tsp harissa paste
2 tbsp flat leaf parsley,
   chopped, plus extra
   to garnish
salt and freshly ground
   black pepper

Method

1. Heat half the oil in a saucepan and fry the onion, garlic and pepper for 5 minutes. Add the giant couscous and fry for 3 more minutes.

2. Pour in the stock and cook for 15 minutes or until it has all been absorbed.

3. Meanwhile, stir the rest of the oil with the paprika and brush it over the prawns. Cook under a preheated grill for 3 minutes on each side or until they turn pink.

4. When the couscous is ready, stir in the harissa and parsley and season to taste with salt and pepper.

5. Serve the prawns with the couscous, garnished with extra parsley sprigs.

Smart tip

Giant couscous is now widely available in supermarkets.

Smart tip

The spaghetti may cook quicker than usual when covered with the steamer, so keep an eye on it.

Cod with tomato spaghetti

Preparation time
5 minutes

Cooking time
12 minutes

Serves 4

Ingredients

4 portions of cod fillet
salt and freshly ground
    black pepper
400 g / 14 oz / 2 cups dried
    spaghetti
3 tbsp olive oil
3 cloves of garlic, crushed
1 dried chilli (chili), chopped
150 g / 5 ½ oz / 1 cup cherry
    tomatoes, halved
2 tbsp pine nuts
a handful of basil leaves

Method

1. Put a large pan of salted water on to boil and set a steamer on top of it. Lay the cod in the steamer basket and season well with salt and pepper. Cook the spaghetti in the water below according to the packet instructions or until al dente.

2. Meanwhile, heat the oil in a large sauté pan and fry the garlic and chilli for 2 minutes. Add half of the cherry tomatoes, then cover the pan and cook for 5 minutes.

3. Stir in the rest of the tomatoes and half of the pine nuts and basil leaves. Season to taste with salt and pepper.

4. Drain the pasta and stir it through the sauce. Divide between four warm plates, then top with the cod and scatter over the rest of the pine nuts and basil.

Baked cauliflower steaks

Preparation time
5 minutes

Cooking time
25 minutes

Serves 4

Ingredients

4 thick slices cauliflower
1 lemon, zest finely grated
2 cloves of garlic, crushed
2 tbsp flat leaf parsley,
    finely chopped
4 tbsp olive oil
4 large potatoes, peeled and
    cubed
4 tbsp butter
4 tbsp milk
salt and freshly ground black
    pepper
50 g / 1 ¾ oz / 2 cups rocket
    (arugula) leaves

Method

1. Preheat the oven to 180°C (160°C fan) / 350F / gas 4.

2. Arrange the cauliflower slices in a single layer in a shallow roasting tin.

3. Stir the lemon zest, garlic and parsley into the oil and brush it over the cauliflower, then pour 50 ml / 2 fl. oz / ¼ cup of cold water into the tin.

4. Bake for 25 minutes or until the cauliflower is tender to the point of a knife.

5. Meanwhile, boil the potatoes in salted water for 15 minutes or until a knife will slide in easily. Drain well, then mash with the butter and milk and season with salt and pepper.

6. Serve the cauliflower with the mash and some rocket on the side.

Smart tip

If the cauliflower starts browning too quickly, cover the tin with foil.

Smart tip

If you have time, soak the wooden skewers in cold water for 20 minutes before using.

Chicken skewers with spaghetti

Preparation time
10 minutes

Cooking time
15 minutes

Serves 4

Ingredients

300 g / 10 ½ oz / 2 cups
  chicken breast, cubed
4 spring onions (scallions), cut
  into short lengths
3 tbsp barbecue sauce

For the spaghetti:
400 g / 14 oz / 2 cups dried
  spaghetti
½ carrot, grated
½ red pepper, grated
3 tbsp basil, shredded
3 tbsp olive oil

Method

1. Preheat the grill to its highest setting and put a pan of salted water on to heat.

2. Thread the chicken and spring onions onto four wooden skewers, then brush with barbecue sauce.

3. Cook the spaghetti in boiling water according to the packet instructions or until al dente.

4. Meanwhile, cook the skewers for 8 minutes, turning occasionally, until the chicken is cooked through.

5. Drain the spaghetti then toss it with the carrot, pepper, basil and oil. Divide between four warm bowls and top each one with a chicken skewer.

Wild mushroom frittata

Preparation time
10 minutes

Cooking time
20 minutes

Serves 6

Ingredients

250 g / 9 oz / 2 ½ cups mixed
wild mushrooms, to include
morels and trompets
de la mort
3 tbsp butter
salt and freshly ground
black pepper
6 large eggs, lightly beaten
fresh chives to garnish

Method

1. Clean the mushrooms with a dry brush to remove any earth. Cut the morels in half and give them a wipe with kitchen paper. Tear the trompets into thick strips.

2. Heat the grill to its highest setting.

3. Heat 2 tbsp of the butter in an ovenproof frying pan, then sauté the mushrooms for 2 minutes. Season with salt and pepper, then continue to cook for 6 minutes or until any liquid that comes out of them has evaporated.

4. Add the rest of the butter to the pan. As soon as it has melted, pour in the eggs and stir well.

5. Reduce the heat to low and cook the eggs, without stirring, until they start to set around the edge of the pan.

6. Put the frying pan under the grill and cook until the top of the frittata is golden brown and the centre is just set.

7. Leave the frittata to cool to room temperature, then cut into wedges and serve garnished with chives.

Smart tip

Don't rinse the
mushrooms with water
as they are absorbent.

Smart tip

This dish really makes the most of inexpensive canned salmon, but also works well with leftover poached salmon.

Salmon tacos with mango salsa

Preparation time
15 minutes

Serves 4

Ingredients

50 g / 1 ¾ oz / 2 cups mixed leaf salad
8 corn taco shells
400 g / 14 oz / 1 ½ cups canned salmon
1 lime, juiced
1 red chilli (chili), finely chopped
4 tbsp soured cream

For the salsa:

1 large mango, peeled and stoned
¼ cucumber
1 red chilli (chili), finely chopped
a small bunch fresh coriander (cilantro), chopped
1 lime, juiced
salt

Method

1. First make the salsa. Cut the mango and cucumber into small cubes and toss with the chilli, coriander and lime juice. Season to taste with salt.

2. Divide the lettuce between the taco shells. Mash the salmon with a fork and stir in the lime juice and chilli.

3. Divide the salmon mixture between the tacos and top with the soured cream, then serve with the mango salsa on the side.

Rib-eye steak with tomatoes

Preparation time
10 minutes

Cooking time
6 minutes

Serves 1

Ingredients

1 large rib-eye steak
salt and freshly ground
    black pepper
1 tbsp olive oil
1 sprig of rosemary
1 clove of garlic, halved
4 cherry tomatoes, halved

Method

1. Put a frying pan over a high heat and season the steak liberally with salt and pepper.

2. Drizzle the oil over the base of the pan then lower in the steak and add the rosemary, garlic and tomatoes, cut side down, next to it.

3. Cook without disturbing for 3 minutes, then turn everything over and cook for another 3 minutes. If you prefer your steak well-done, cook it for another 2-3 minutes on each side.

4. Wrap the steak in a double layer of foil and leave to rest for 5 minutes, then serve with the tomatoes.

Smart tip

This recipe can be doubled or quadrupled to feed more people, but don't overcrowd the frying pan.

Smart tip

This fat-free cooking method works well for bream and mullet too.

Steamed sea bass with lemon and lime leaves

Preparation time
5 minutes

Cooking time
10 minutes

Serves 2

Ingredients

2 small sea bass, heads and
    skin removed
1 lemon, sliced
4 kaffir lime leaves
salt and freshly ground
    black pepper

Method

1. Preheat a steamer. Lay the sea bass on a plate that will fit in the steamer and arrange the lemon slices and lime leaves on top. Season with salt and pepper.

2. Steam the fish for 10 minutes or until the flesh pulls away easily from the bones.

Jerk chicken and pineapple kebabs

Preparation time
10 minutes

Cooking time
10 minutes

Serves 2

Ingredients

300 g / 10 ½ oz / 2 cups chicken breast, cubed
½ pineapple, peeled, cored and cut into chunks
1 tbsp jerk paste
2 tbsp vegetable oil

Method

1. Preheat the grill to its highest setting.
2. Thread the chicken and pineapple onto four metal skewers.
3. Stir the jerk paste into the oil and brush all over the chicken and pineapple.
4. Grill the kebabs for 10 minutes, turning regularly, or until the chicken is cooked through and toasted at the edges.

Smart tip

If you have time, leave the kebabs to marinate for 10 minutes for a richer taste.

Smart tip

Don't add the mozzarella too soon as it won't keep its shape.

Farfalle with tomatoes, mushrooms and bacon

Preparation time
5 minutes

Cooking time
12 minutes

Serves 4

Ingredients

400 g / 14 oz / 3 cups dried
  farfalle
2 tbsp olive oil
2 rashers smoked streaky
  bacon, chopped
2 cloves of garlic, crushed
150 g / 5 ½ oz / 2 cups button
  mushrooms, halved
  and sliced
150 g / 5 ½ oz / 1 cup cherry
  tomatoes, halved
1 mozzarella ball, torn into
  small chunks
a handful of basil leaves
freshly ground black pepper

Method

1. Cook the pasta in boiling, salted water according to the packet instructions or until al dente.

2. While the pasta is cooking, heat the oil in a sauté pan and fry the bacon for 2 minutes. Stir in the garlic and mushrooms and sauté for 5 minutes. Stir in the tomatoes and warm through.

3. When the pasta is ready, drain it well and add it to the sauté pan. Toss well, adding the mozzarella, then divide between four warm bowls. Garnish with basil leaves and season with freshly ground black pepper.

Breaded veal with lemon and thyme

Preparation time
15 minutes

Cooking time
10 minutes

Serves 3

Ingredients

4 tbsp plain (all-purpose) flour
1 egg, beaten
75 g / 2 ½ oz / ½ cup panko breadcrumbs
3 tbsp Parmesan, finely grated
3 veal escalopes
3 tbsp butter
2 cloves of garlic, unpeeled
1 lemon, zest finely pared
a small bunch of thyme
potato wedges to serve

Method

1. Put the flour and egg in separate bowls and mix the panko crumbs and Parmesan in a third.
2. Dip the escalopes alternately in the flour, egg and breadcrumbs and shake off any excess.
3. Heat the butter in a large frying pan that will hold the escalopes in a single layer. Add the garlic cloves, lemon zest and half of the thyme, then cut the lemon into slices.
4. Lower the escalopes gently into the pan and tuck the lemon slices into any gaps. Let the veal cook without disturbing for 5 minutes.
5. Turn the escalopes and lemon slices over and fry for 5 minutes on the other side, then garnish with fresh thyme and serve with potato wedges.

Smart tip

The whole garlic cloves
will enhance the butter
without burning, but
can be discarded
before serving.

King prawn and red mullet risotto

Preparation time
5 minutes

Cooking time
25 minutes

Serves 2

Ingredients

1 litre / 1 pint 15 fl. oz / 4 cups
    fish stock
2 tbsp olive oil
1 onion, finely chopped
2 cloves of garlic, sliced
150 g / 5 ½ oz / ¾ cup risotto
    rice
100 g / 3 ½ oz / ⅔ cup raw
    king prawns, peeled
4 red mullet fillets, halved
salt and freshly ground
    black pepper

Method

1. Heat the stock in a saucepan.

2. Heat the olive oil in a sauté pan and gently fry the onion for 5 minutes without browning. Add the garlic and cook for 2 more minutes, then stir in the rice. When the rice is well coated with the oil, add two ladles of the hot stock.

3. Cook, stirring occasionally, until most of the stock has been absorbed before adding the next two ladles. Continue in this way for around 15 minutes or until the rice is just tender.

4. Stir in the prawns and mullet, then cover the pan and take off the heat to rest for 4 minutes.

5. Uncover the pan and season well with salt and pepper, then spoon into warm bowls and serve.

Chicken burgers with tomato and cucumber salad

Preparation time
24 minutes

Cooking time
6 minutes

Serves 4

Ingredients

600 g / 1 lb 5 ½ oz / 4 cups
  chicken thigh, chopped
1 clove of garlic, crushed
1 tbsp lemon zest,
  finely grated
3 tbsp Parmesan,
  finely grated
a small bunch basil, chopped
2 tbsp olive oil

For the salad:
3 large tomatoes, sliced
½ cucumber, sliced
a handful of basil leaves
2 tbsp red wine vinegar
3 tbsp olive oil
lemon wedges to garnish

Method

1. Put the chicken, garlic, lemon zest, Parmesan and basil in a food processor and pulse until it forms a ball.

2. Shape the mixture into 12 small burgers and transfer to the freezer for 15 minutes to firm up.

3. Heat the oil in a large frying pan and fry the burgers for 3 minutes on each side or until cooked through and golden brown.

4. Arrange the tomato, cucumber and basil on four plates and drizzle with vinegar and oil. Serve with the burgers and lemon wedges to garnish.

Smart tip

Chilling in the freezer
rather than the
fridge speeds up
the process.

Smart tip

Using leftover boiled
potatoes cuts out
1 hour of soaking,
30 minutes of drying

Fish and chips

Preparation time
15 minutes

Cooking time
11 minutes

Serves 4

Ingredients

sunflower oil for deep-frying
200 g / 7 oz / 1 ⅓ cups plain
    (all-purpose) flour
2 tbsp olive oil
250 ml / 9 fl. oz / 1 cup pale
    ale
4 portions pollock fillet
400 g / 14 oz / 2 cups leftover
    boiled potatoes,
    cut into chips
lime wedges and spicy tartare
    sauce to serve

Method

1. Heat the oil in a deep fat fryer, according to the manufacturer's instructions, to a temperature of 180°C (350F).

2. Sieve the flour into a bowl then whisk in the oil and ale until smoothly combined.

3. Dip the fish in the batter and fry for 6 minutes or until golden brown. Transfer the fish to a kitchen paper lined bowl and increase the fryer temperature to 190°C (375F).

4. Fry the chips for 5 minutes or until crisp and golden brown. Drain the chips of excess oil and serve with the fish, lime wedges and spicy tartare sauce.

Veal burgers

Preparation time
15 minutes

Cooking time
8 minutes

Serves 4

Ingredients

450 g / 1 lb / 2 cups veal
 mince
2 tbsp double (heavy) cream
1 tsp Dijon mustard
salt and freshly ground
 black pepper
2 tbsp sunflower oil
4 burger buns, halved
 horizontally
4 tbsp mayonnaise
4 lettuce leaves
½ red onion, sliced
a handful of tarragon shoots

Method

1. Mix the mince with the cream and mustard and season generously with salt and pepper, then knead lightly until sticky. Divide the mixture into four and press each piece into a ring mould to get an even shape.

2. Heat the oil in a frying pan then fry the burgers for 8 minutes, turning every 2 minutes.

3. Toast the burger buns, then spread the bases with mayonnaise. Top each one with a lettuce leaf and a burger, then arrange the onion and tarragon shoots on top.

4. Put the lids on the buns and serve immediately.

Smart tip

If you can't find
ready-minced veal, ask
the butcher to mince
it for you.

Smart tip

Make sure the griddle pan is really hot so the melon browns without softening too much.

Lamb fillet with griddled melon

Preparation time
5 minutes

Cooking time
6 minutes

Serves 1

Ingredients

1 portion of lamb fillet
salt and freshly ground
   black pepper
2 tbsp olive oil
3 thin slices melon
1 tsp pink peppercorns
1 tbsp runny honey

Method

1. Put a frying pan over a high heat and season the lamb liberally with salt and pepper.

2. Drizzle 1 tbsp of the oil over the base of the pan then add the lamb.

3. Cook without disturbing for 3 minutes, then turn it over and cook for another 3 minutes. If you prefer your lamb well done, cook it for another 2–3 minutes on each side.

4. While the lamb is cooking, brush the melon slices with the rest of the oil and sear in a hot griddle pan.

5. Transfer the lamb to a warm plate and cover with foil. Stir the peppercorns and honey into the frying pan and add any juices that come out of the lamb.

6. Serve the melon slices with the lamb and spoon over the pan juices.

Sesame meatball pasta

Preparation time
15 minutes

Cooking time
15 minutes

Serves 4

Ingredients

225 g / 8 oz / 1 cup minced
  lamb
225 g / 8 oz / 1 cup sausage
  meat
50 g / 2 oz / ⅔ cup fresh white
  breadcrumbs
3 tbsp hummus
2 tbsp flat leaf parsley,
  finely chopped
salt and freshly ground
  black pepper
4 tbsp sesame seeds
4 tbsp olive oil
400 g / 14 oz / 4 cups dried
  fusilli
8 cherry tomatoes, quartered
50 g / 1 ¾ oz / ½ cup
  Parmesan, finely grated
basil leaves to garnish

Method

1. Knead the lamb mince, sausage meat, breadcrumbs, hummus and parsley together and season with salt and pepper. Shape the mixture into meatballs and roll in the sesame seeds to coat.

2. Heat half of the oil in a frying pan and fry the meatballs for 15 minutes or until cooked through, turning occasionally.

3. Meanwhile, boil the pasta in salted water according to the packet instructions or until al dente.

4. Drain the pasta then toss it with the meatballs and tomatoes and dress with the rest of the oil. Divide between four warm bowls and sprinkle generously with Parmesan. Garnish with basil leaves.

Smart tip
Look out for lamb sausage meat if you would rather keep the dish pork free.

Smart tip

When corn on the cob is out of season, use tinned sweetcorn and reduce the cooking time by 10 minutes.

Speedy chorizo, potato and sweetcorn stew

Preparation time
5 minutes

Cooking time
25 minutes

Serves 4

Ingredients

2 tbsp olive oil
250 g / 9 oz / 1 ⅔ cups mini
   cooking chorizo
4 spring onions (scallions),
   cut into short lengths
1 tsp Cayenne pepper
2 corn cobs, cut into
   thick slices
400 ml / 7 fl. oz / 1 ⅔ cups
   tomato passata
2 leftover boiled potatoes,
   cut into wedges
1 lime, cut into chunks
2 tbsp coriander (cilantro),
   chopped

Method

1. Heat the oil in a saucepan and fry the chorizo and spring onions for 3 minutes. Stir in the Cayenne and cook for 1 more minute, then stir in the corn and passata.

2. Simmer for 15 minutes, then stir in the potatoes and simmer for 5 more minutes.

3. Divide between four warm bowls and garnish with lime chunks and coriander.

Scallop brochettes

Preparation time
10 minutes

Cooking time
4 minutes

Serves 2

Ingredients

16 scallops, shelled and
  corals removed
4 lemongrass stems
2 tbsp lime juice
1 tbsp fish sauce
1 tbsp caster (superfine)
  sugar
1 red chilli (chili), deseeded
  and sliced
steamed rice to serve

Method

1. Preheat the grill to its highest setting.
2. Thread four scallops onto each lemongrass stem.
3. Stir the lime juice, fish sauce and sugar together, then brush the mixture over the scallops.
4. Grill the scallops for 2 minutes on each side or until lightly toasted and only just cooked in the centre.
5. Sprinkle with chilli and serve with steamed rice.

Smart tip
Don't overcook the
scallops or they
will toughen.

Smart tip

If you prefer a less spicy curry, remove the chilli (chili) seeds or serve with a dollop of natural yoghurt.

Chicken jalfrezi

Preparation time
5 minutes

Cooking time
20 minutes

Serves 4

Ingredients

2 tbsp sunflower oil
1 onion, sliced
2 cloves of garlic, crushed
1 tbsp fresh root ginger,
    finely chopped
2 green chillies (chilies),
    finely chopped
4 chicken breasts, cubed
2 red peppers, deseeded
    and sliced
2 tbsp jalfrezi spice paste
400 ml / 7 fl. oz / 1 ⅔ cups
    tomato passata
salt
coriander (cilantro) sprigs
    to garnish
basmati rice and naan bread
    to serve

Method

1. Heat the oil in a sauté pan and fry the onion for 5 minutes
   to soften. Add the garlic, ginger and chillies and fry for
   2 more minutes.

2. Add the chicken, peppers and spice paste to the pan and
   stir-fry until the chicken is lightly browned.

3. Pour in the passata and bring to the boil, then reduce the
   heat and simmer for 10 minutes or until the chicken is
   cooked through.

4. Taste the sauce and add salt if needed, then garnish with
   coriander and serve with rice and naan bread.

Lentil and smoked haddock salad

Preparation time
10 minutes

Serves 4

Ingredients

400 g / 14 oz / 2 ⅔ cups
    canned puy lentils,
    drained and rinsed
2 shallots, sliced
4 tbsp olive oil
1 lemon, juiced
2 tbsp chives, chopped
2 tbsp flat leaf parsley,
    chopped
salt and freshly ground
    black pepper
225 g / 8 oz / 1 ½ cups
    smoked haddock fillet,
    thinly sliced

Method

1. Toss the lentils with the shallots, oil, lemon juice and herbs, then season to taste with salt and pepper.

2. Divide between four bowls and garnish with smoked haddock.

Smart tip

You can now buy ready-to-eat lentils in plastic pouches as well as cans.

Smart tip

Cut the end of the rosemary stalks off on the diagonal to make threading easier.

Veal, cheese and rosemary skewers

Preparation time
15 minutes

Cooking time
8 minutes

Serves 4

Ingredients

8 thin veal escalopes
8 slices Emmental cheese
8 sage leaves
4 long woody rosemary
   sprigs
mixed salad leaves to serve

Method

1. Preheat the grill to its highest setting.
2. Top each escalope with a slice of cheese and a sage leaf, then roll them up.
3. Remove most of the leaves from the rosemary sprigs, then thread two veal rolls onto each skewer.
4. Cook the skewers under the grill for 8 minutes, turning occasionally.
5. Serve with mixed salad leaves.

Farfalle with prosciutto, feta and pistachios

Preparation time
5 minutes

Cooking time
12 minutes

Serves 4

Ingredients

400 g / 14 oz / 3 cups dried farfalle
5 tbsp olive oil
3 tbsp pistachio nuts
75 g / 2 ½ oz / ¾ cup feta, cubed
6 slices prosciutto, chopped

Method

1. Cook the pasta in boiling, salted water according to the packet instructions or until al dente.
2. Meanwhile, put the oil and pistachio nuts in a mini food processor and pulse to chop. Add the feta and pulse a few more times. Stir in the prosciutto.
3. When the pasta is ready, reserve a few tbsp of the cooking water and drain the rest. Stir in the pistachio mixture, adding a splash of the cooking water if it looks dry.
4. Divide between four warm bowls and serve immediately.

Smart tip

This recipe also works well with hazelnuts (cobnuts).

Smart tip

When scrubbing the mussels, discard any that won't close when tapped.

Mussels with white wine and parsley

Preparation time
5 minutes

Cooking time
18 minutes

Serves 4

Ingredients

2 tbsp olive oil
1 onion, sliced
1 celery stick, sliced
3 cloves of garlic, finely
   chopped
250 ml / 9 fl. oz / 1 cup dry
   white wine
2 litres / 3 pints 7 fl. oz /
   8 cups live mussels,
   scrubbed
3 tbsp flat leaf parsley,
   chopped
freshly ground black pepper

Method

1. Heat the oil in a large saucepan and gently fry the onion, celery and garlic for 5 minutes. Pour in the wine and bring to the boil, then reduce by half.

2. Add the mussels to the pan, cover with a lid and leave to steam for 8 minutes or until they have all opened, shaking the pan halfway through.

3. Stir in the parsley and season with black pepper, then serve immediately.

Stir-fried duck with mangetout and sesame

Preparation time
5 minutes

Cooking time
10 minutes

Serves 4

Ingredients

2 tbsp vegetable oil
3 duck breasts, skinned and sliced
200 g / 7 oz / 2 cups mangetout
2 tbsp runny honey
2 tbsp light soy sauce
2 tbsp orange juice
1 tsp sesame oil
2 tbsp sesame seeds

Method

1. Heat the oil in a large wok and stir-fry the duck slices for 3 minutes.
2. Add the mangetout to the pan and stir-fry for 3 more minutes.
3. Stir the honey, soy sauce and orange juice together, then pour the mixture into the wok and stir-fry until reduced to a sticky glaze.
4. Sprinkle in the sesame oil and seeds, then serve immediately.

Smart tip

Keep stirring the
ingredients once the
honey goes in, as it has
a tendency to catch.

Smart tip
Look out for pouches of
microwave rice in the
supermarket.

Speedy kedgeree

Cooking time
30 minutes

Serves 6

Ingredients

600 ml / 1 pint / 2 ½ cups
  whole (full-fat) milk
450 g / 1 lb smoked haddock
  fillet
50 g / 1 ¾ oz / ¼ cup butter
1 large onion, finely chopped
2 garlic cloves, crushed
2 tbsp mild curry powder
250 g / 9 oz / 2 cups
  microwave rice
2 tbsp flat leaf parsley,
  chopped

Method

1. Bring the milk to a simmer then pour it into a dish with the smoked haddock. Cover the dish with clingfilm and leave to steep for 8 minutes.

2. Drain off and reserve the milk and flake the haddock, discarding any skin and bones.

3. Meanwhile, melt the butter in a large saucepan and fry the onions for 5 minutes, then add the garlic and cook for 2 more minutes.

4. Add the curry powder and rice and stir to coat in the butter, then add 3 tbsp of the haddock milk. When the liquid starts to bubble, stir in the microwave rice and cook for 3 minutes or until all the liquid has been absorbed.

5. Stir in the flaked haddock then divide between six warm bowls and sprinkle with parsley.

Smart tip

Be careful not to
over-whip the cream or
it will go grainy.

White chocolate refrigerator cakes

Preparation time
10 minutes

Cooking time
5 minutes

Freezing time
15 minutes

Makes 6

Ingredients

300 g / 10 ½ oz / 2 cups white
    chocolate, chopped
100 g / 3 ½ oz / ½ cup butter
100 g / 3 ½ oz / ½ cup caster
    (superfine) sugar
3 medium egg yolks
250 g / 9 oz / 1 ⅔ cups
    coconut biscuits
300 ml / 10 ½ fl. oz / 1 ¼ cups
    double (heavy) cream,
    whipped
150 g / 5 ½ oz / 1 cup
    strawberries, halved

Method

1. Melt the chocolate and butter together over a low heat in a saucepan, then remove from the heat.

2. Whisk the sugar and egg yolks together until pale and thick, then fold in the chocolate mixture until smoothly combined.

3. Reserve two biscuits for decoration, then put the rest in a sandwich bag and crush with a rolling pin. Fold the crushed biscuits into the chocolate mixture.

4. Pack six ring moulds with the mixture and level the tops. Transfer the moulds to the freezer to firm up for 15 minutes.

5. Unmould the cakes and top with whipped cream, strawberries and the reserved biscuits crumbled over the top.

Pineapple and vanilla syrup cakes

Preparation time
15 minutes

Cooking time
15 minutes

Makes 8

Ingredients

100 g / 3 ½ oz / ⅔ cup
   self-raising flour
1 tsp baking powder
100 g / 3 ½ oz / ½ cup caster
   (superfine) sugar
100 g / 3 ½ oz / ½ cup butter
2 large eggs
1 tsp vanilla extract
coconut ice cream to serve

For the pineapple:

100 ml / 3 ½ fl. oz / ½ cup
   pineapple juice
100 g / 3 ½ oz / ½ cup caster
   (superfine) sugar
1 vanilla pod, split in half
   lengthways
½ pineapple, peeled and cut
   into chunks

Method

1. Preheat the oven to 180°C (160°C fan) / 350F / gas 4 and grease and line a Swiss roll tin.

2. Put the flour, baking powder, sugar, butter, eggs and vanilla extract in a large mixing bowl and whisk together with an electric whisk for 4 minutes or until pale and well whipped.

3. Spoon the mixture into the tin and spread into an even layer with a palette knife.

4. Bake for 15 minutes or until the cake is springy to the touch.

5. While the cake is cooking, put the pineapple juice, sugar and vanilla pod in a small saucepan. Stir over a low heat until the sugar dissolves, then bring to a simmer. Stir in the pineapple chunks and simmer for 3 minutes, then turn off the heat.

6. Turn the cake out onto a piece of greaseproof paper and use a round cookie cutter to cut out eight circles. Top each cake circle with pineapple pieces and spoon over a little of the warm syrup. Serve with coconut ice cream.

Smart tip

Freeze any cake trimmings to use in trifles.

Smart tip

Make sure the egg white is smoothly combined with no lumps visible.

Whipped chocolate mousse

Preparation time
25 minutes

Cooking time
5 minutes

Serves 4

Ingredients

200 g / 7 oz / ¾ cup double (heavy) cream
200 g / 7 oz / 1 ⅓ cups milk chocolate, chopped
2 large egg whites
4 tbsp caster (superfine) sugar

Method

1. Heat the cream in a pan to simmering point, then pour it over the chocolate and stir until smooth.

2. Cool in the freezer for 15 minutes.

3. Meanwhile, whip the egg whites until stiff then whisk in the sugar.

4. Stir a big spoonful of the egg white into the cooled chocolate mixture, then fold in the rest with a big metal spoon, keeping as many of the air bubbles intact as possible.

5. Spoon the mousse into a piping bag fitted with a large star nozzle. Pipe a big swirl of mousse into four chilled bowls and serve immediately.

Strawberry and rhubarb muesli crumbles

Preparation time
5 minutes

Cooking time
25 minutes

Makes 6

Ingredients

2 rhubarb stalks, chopped
150 g / 5 ½ oz / 1 cup
  strawberries, sliced
3 tbsp caster (superfine)
  sugar
150 g / 5 ½ oz / 1 ½ cups
  muesli
6 scoops vanilla ice cream

Method

1. Preheat the oven to 180°C (160°C fan) / 350F / gas 4.

2. Mix the rhubarb and strawberries with the caster sugar and divide them between six ramekin dishes.

3. Top with the muesli then bake for 25 minutes. Top each crumble with a scoop of vanilla ice cream and serve immediately.

Smart tip

Muesli makes a great speedy crumble topping – try it with any soft fruits.

Smart tip

Serve hot from the grill or chill, ready to serve cold later.

Speedy summer fruit gratin

Preparation time
5 minutes

Cooking time
15 minute

Serves 4

Ingredients

450 ml / 12 ½ fl. oz / 1 ¾ cups whole (full-fat) milk
4 large egg yolks
75 g / 2 ½ oz / ⅓ cup caster (superfine) sugar
2 tsp cornflour (cornstarch)
1 tsp vanilla extract
100 g / 3 ½ oz / ⅔ cup raspberries
100 g / 3 ½ oz / ⅔ cup strawberries, sliced
2 tbsp icing (confectioners') sugar

Method

1. Preheat the grill to its highest setting.

2. Pour the milk into a saucepan and bring to simmering point. Meanwhile, whisk the egg yolks with the caster sugar, cornflour and vanilla extract until thick.

3. Gradually incorporate the hot milk, whisking all the time, then scrape the mixture back into the saucepan. Stir the custard over a low heat until it thickens.

4. Divide the fruit between four individual gratin dishes and pour over the custard.

5. Sprinkle the top with icing sugar and cook for 1 minute under the grill to caramelise the top.

Chocolate and nut samosas

Preparation time
15 minutes

Cooking time
15 minutes

Serves 6

Ingredients

225 g / 8 oz filo pastry

100 g / 3 ½ oz / ½ cup butter, melted

200 g / 7 oz / 1 ⅓ cups dark chocolate (minimum 60 % cocoa solids), finely chopped

75 g / 2 ½ oz / ½ cup almonds, chopped

icing (confectioners') sugar to dust

Method

1. Preheat the oven to 180°C (160°C fan) / 355F / gas 4 and grease a large baking tray.

2. Cut the filo sheets in half then take one halved sheet and brush it with melted butter.

3. Mix the chocolate and almonds together. Add a tablespoon of the mixture at one end of the sheet and fold the corner over, then triangle-fold it up.

4. Transfer the samosa to the baking tray and repeat with the rest of the filo and chocolate, then brush the triangles with any leftover butter.

5. Bake for 15 minutes or until the pastry is crisp and golden brown. Serve dusted with icing sugar.

Smart tip

Tuck the ends of the pastry into the pocket formed by the filo for a neat finish.

Smart tip

This recipe also works well with raspberries in place of the redcurrants.

Fromage frais with redcurrants

Preparation time
10 minutes

Serves 4

Ingredients

150 g / 5 ½ oz / 1 cup
  redcurrants
2 tbsp caster (superfine)
  sugar
300 ml / 10 ½ fl. oz / 1 ¼ cups
  fromage frais
3 tbsp icing (confectioners')
  sugar

Method

1. Put half of the redcurrants in a mini food processor with the caster sugar and purée until smooth. Pass through a sieve to remove the seeds, then stir in the rest of the redcurrants.

2. Stir the fromage frais and icing sugar together and divide between four small bowls. Top with the redcurrants and serve immediately.

Mirabelle plum clafoutis

Preparation time
5 minutes

Cooking time
25 minutes

Serves 6

Ingredients

75 g / 2 ½ oz / ⅓ cup butter, melted
75 g / 2 ½ oz / ⅓ cup caster (superfine) sugar
300 ml / 10 ½ fl. oz / 1 ¼ cups whole milk
2 large eggs
50 g / 1 ¾ oz / ⅓ cup plain (all-purpose) flour
a pinch of salt
2 tbsp ground almonds
300 g / 10 ½ oz / 2 cups mirabelle plums

Method

1. Preheat the oven to 190°C (170°C fan) / 375F / gas 5.

2. Brush a little of the butter around the inside of a large baking dish then add a spoonful of the caster sugar and shake to coat the dish.

3. Whisk together the milk and eggs with the rest of the butter. Sift the flour into a mixing bowl with a pinch of salt, then stir in the ground almonds and the rest of the sugar. Make a well in the middle of the dry ingredients and gradually whisk in the liquid, incorporating all the flour from round the outside until you have a lump-free batter.

4. Arrange the plums in the prepared baking dish and pour over the batter. Bake the clafoutis for 25 minutes or until a skewer inserted in the centre comes out clean.

Smart tip

Choose a wide, shallow baking dish to cook the clafoutis as quickly as possible.

Smart tip
Try replacing the apples
with peeled and
diced pears for an
alternative taste.

Apple and cinnamon crumble

Preparation time
5 minutes

Cooking time
25 minutes

Serves 6

Ingredients

2 large bramley apples,
   peeled, cored and
   chopped
2 eating apples, peeled,
   cored and chopped
4 tbsp caster (superfine)
   sugar
75 g / 2 ½ oz / ⅓ cup butter
50 g / 1 ¾ oz / ⅓ cup plain
   (all-purpose) flour
25 g / 1 oz / ¼ cup ground
   almonds
2 tsp ground cinnamon
40 g / 1 ½ oz / ¼ cup light
   brown sugar

Method

1. Preheat the oven to 180°C (160°C fan) / 350F / gas 4.

2. Mix the apples with the sugar and arrange in a foil baking tray.

3. Rub the butter into the flour and stir in the ground almonds,
   cinnamon and brown sugar. Squeeze a handful of the mixture
   into a clump and then crumble it over the fruit. Use up the rest
   of the topping in the same way, then shake the dish to level
   the top.

4. Bake the crumble for 25 minutes or until the topping is
   golden brown.

Roasted stone fruit

Preparation time
5 minutes

Cooking time
15 minutes

Serves 4

Ingredients

2 peaches, halved and stoned
2 plums, halved and stoned
4 apricots, halved and stoned
2 tbsp butter
3 tbsp runny honey
a few sprigs of thyme

Method

1. Preheat the oven to 180°C (160°C fan) / 350F / gas 4.
2. Arrange the fruit cut side up in a roasting tin lined with greaseproof paper. Add a small knob of butter to the cavity of each one, then drizzle with honey and scatter over the thyme.
3. Bake for 15 minutes or until the fruit is tender to the point of a knife.

Smart tip

Lining the roasting tin with greaseproof paper makes the washing up quicker.

Smart tip

The cardamom pods are for decoration and taste, but shouldn't be eaten.

Mango and cardamom cheesecake pots

Preparation time
25 minutes

Cooking time
5 minutes

Makes 6

Ingredients

200 g / 7 oz / 1 ⅓ cups
  digestive biscuits, crushed
50 g / 1 ¾ oz / ¼ cup butter,
  melted
400 g / 14 oz / 2 cups
  mascarpone
4 tbsp icing (confectioners')
  sugar
1 tsp vanilla extract
2 limes, juiced
3 tbsp runny honey
2 tbsp white rum
10 cardamom pods
1 mango, peeled, stoned
  and chopped
basil sprigs to garnish

Method

1. Mix the biscuit crumbs with the butter and press into an even layer in the bottom of six glasses.

2. Whisk together the mascarpone, icing sugar and vanilla extract with half of the lime juice until smooth. Spoon the cheesecake mixture on top of the biscuit bases and level the tops.

3. Put the rest of the lime juice in a small saucepan with the honey, rum and cardamom. Bring to the boil, then leave to infuse for 5 minutes.

4. Stir in the mango and spoon the mixture over the cheesecakes. Garnish with basil and serve.

Chocolate torte

Preparation time
5 minutes

Cooking time
25 minutes

Serves 8

Ingredients

110g / 4 oz ⅔ cup dark
chocolate (minimum 60 %
cocoa solids), chopped
85 g / 3 oz / ¾ cup
unsweetened cocoa
powder, plus extra
for dusting
225 g / 8 oz / 1 cup butter
450 g / 1 lb / 2 ½ cups light
brown sugar
4 large eggs
110 g / 4 oz / 1 cup ground
almonds
icing (confectioners') sugar
for dusting

Method

1. Preheat the oven to 170°C (150°C fan) / 340F / gas 3 and oil
   and line a 28 cm (11 in) round tart tin.

2. Melt the chocolate, cocoa and butter together in a saucepan.

3. Whisk the sugar and eggs together with an electric whisk for
   2 minutes or until very light and creamy.

4. Pour in the chocolate mixture and ground almonds, then fold
   everything together until evenly mixed.

5. Scrape into the tin and bake for 25 minutes or until the
   outside is set, but the centre is still quite soft, as it will continue
   to cook as it cools.

6. Dust with icing sugar before serving.

Smart tip

Use a solid rather than
loose-bottomed tart tin
or the mixture might
run through.

Strawberry verrines

Preparation time
20 minutes

Serves 4

Ingredients

200 g / 7 oz / ¾ cup Madeira
  cake, sliced
4 tbsp crème de cacao
400 ml / 14 fl. oz / 1 ⅔ cup
  custard
150 g / 5 ½ oz / 1 cup
  strawberries, sliced
mint sprigs to garnish

Method

1. Arrange half of the cake slices in the bottom of four glasses
   and drizzle with half of the crème de cacao.

2. Spoon half of the custard on top then add a layer of
   strawberry slices.

3. Repeat steps 1 and 2 with the remaining ingredients and
   garnish with mint sprigs.

Orange liqueur soufflés

Preparation time
18 minutes

Cooking time
12 minutes

Serves 4

Ingredients

50 g / 1 ¾ oz / ¼ cup butter
3 tbsp caster (superfine)
   sugar
175 ml / 6 ½ fl. oz / ¾ cup
   whole milk
1 orange, zest finely grated
25 g / 1 oz / ⅙ cup plain
   (all-purpose) flour
4 large eggs, separated
3 tbsp orange liqueur

Method

1. Preheat the oven to 220°C (200°C fan) / 425F / gas 8 and put a kettle of water on to boil.

2. Use half of the butter to grease four ramekins, then sprinkle the insides with a tablespoon of the sugar.

3. Put the milk, remaining sugar and orange zest in a small saucepan and bring to simmering point. Meanwhile, melt the rest of the butter in a small saucepan. Stir in the flour then gradually incorporate the milk, stirring continuously to avoid any lumps forming. When the mixture starts to bubble, take the pan off the heat and beat in the egg yolks and orange liqueur.

4. Whip the egg whites with an electric whisk until they form stiff peaks. Stir a tablespoon of the egg whites into the egg yolk mixture to loosen, it then carefully fold in the rest of the egg white, retaining as much air as possible.

5. Divide the mixture between the cups and level the tops with a palette knife. Run the tip of your thumb round the inside rim to create a lip as this will help the soufflés to rise evenly.

6. Transfer the cups to a roasting tin and pour enough boiling water around them to come halfway up the sides. Bake for 12 minutes or until they are well risen and golden brown. Serve immediately.

Smart tip

Boiling water in the tin starts cooking the soufflés straight away and creates the best rise.

Smart tip
Cooking the butter first
helps to enrich the dish.

Individual cherry clafoutis

Preparation time
10 minutes

Cooking time
20 minutes

Makes 8

Ingredients

75 g / 2 ½ oz / ⅓ cup butter
75 g / 2 ½ oz / ⅓ cup caster
  (superfine) sugar
300 ml / 10 ½ fl. oz / 1 ¼ cups
  whole milk
2 large eggs
50 g / 1 ¾ oz / ⅓ cup plain
  (all-purpose) flour
a pinch of salt
2 tbsp ground almonds
300 g / 10 ½ oz / 2 cups
  cherries, stoned

Method

1. Preheat the oven to 190°C (170°C fan) / 375F / gas 5.

2. Melt the butter in a saucepan and cook over a low heat until it starts to smell nutty.

3. Brush a little of the butter around the inside of eight ramekins then sprinkle with a little of the caster sugar and shake to coat.

4. Whisk together the milk and eggs in the pan with the rest of the butter.

5. Sift the flour into a mixing bowl with a pinch of salt, then stir in the ground almonds and the rest of the sugar.

6. Make a well in the middle of the dry ingredients and gradually whisk in the liquid, incorporating all the flour from round the outside until you have a lump-free batter.

7. Arrange the cherries in the prepared ramekins, then pour in the batter. Bake for 20 minutes or until a skewer inserted in the centre comes out clean.

Tiramisu

Preparation time
20 minutes

Serves 6

Ingredients

600 ml / 1 pint / 2 ½ cups
  double (heavy) cream
300 g / 10 ½ oz / 1 ⅓ cups
  mascarpone
4 tbsp icing (confectioners')
  sugar
100 ml / 3 ½ fl. oz / ½ cup
  Marsala wine
100 ml / 3 ½ fl. oz / ½ cup
  strong filter coffee, cooled
300 g / 10 ½ oz / 2 ½ cups
  sponge fingers
unsweetened cocoa powder
  for dusting

Method

1. Put the cream, mascarpone and sugar in a bowl with half of the Marsala and whip with an electric whisk until it holds its shape.

2. Mix the rest of the Marsala with the coffee. Dip half of the sponge fingers in the coffee mixture and divide between six glasses. Spread half of the cream mixture over the top.

3. Dip the rest of the sponge fingers in the coffee and arrange on top.

4. Spoon the rest of the cream mixture on top and dust with cocoa.

Smart tip

Serve straight away or
chill in the fridge for
later and let the
taste develop.

Smart tip

Squeezing and
crumbling the topping
gives the best texture.

Individual rhubarb crumbles

Preparation time
10 minutes

Cooking time
20 minutes

Makes 4

Ingredients

300 g / 9 oz / 2 cups rhubarb,
cut into short lengths
4 tbsp caster (superfine)
sugar
75 g / 2 ½ oz / ⅓ cup butter
50 g / 1 ¾ oz / ⅓ cup plain
(all-purpose) flour
25 g / 1 oz / ¼ cup ground
almonds
40 g / 1 ½ oz / ¼ cup light
brown sugar

Method

1. Preheat the oven to 180°C (160°C fan) / 350F / gas 4.

2. Put the rhubarb in a saucepan with the sugar and a splash of water and cook with the lid on for 5 minutes or until softened.

3. Meanwhile, rub the butter into the flour and stir in the ground almonds and brown sugar.

4. Divide the cooked rhubarb between four gratin dishes.

5. Squeeze a handful of the crumble mixture into a clump and then crumble it over the rhubarb. Use up the rest of the topping in the same way, then shake the dishes to level the tops.

6. Bake the crumbles for 20 minutes or until the tops are golden brown.

Strawberry and mint tartare

Preparation time
20 minutes

Serves 2

Ingredients

150 g / 5 ½ oz / 1 cup
   strawberries, hulled
2 tbsp runny honey
1 tbsp balsamic vinegar
1 tbsp mint leaves, finely
   chopped
biscuit fingers to serve

Method

1. Finely dice the strawberries and mix with the honey, vinegar and mint.
2. Leave to macerate for 15 minutes, then spoon into two dishes and serve with biscuit fingers.

Smart tip

Macerating the fruit really brings out the strawberry taste.

Smart tip

Dulce de leche can usually be found in the dessert sauces aisle of the supermarket.

Banana, toffee and coconut crumble

Preparation time
8 minutes

Cooking time
20 minutes

Serves 4

Ingredients

4 bananas, peeled
6 tbsp dulce de leche
75 g / 2 ½ oz / ⅓ cup butter
50 g / 1 ¾ oz / ⅓ cup plain
   (all-purpose) flour
50 g / 1 ¾ oz / ½ cup
   desiccated coconut
40 g / 1 ½ oz / ¼ cup light
   brown sugar

Method

1. Preheat the oven to 180°C (160°C fan) / 350F / gas 4.
2. Arrange the bananas in a single layer in a small baking dish and spoon over the dulce de leche.
3. Rub the butter into the flour and stir in the desiccated coconut and sugar.
4. Take a handful of the topping and squeeze it into a clump, then crumble it over the bananas.
5. Repeat with the rest of the crumble mixture then bake for 20 minutes or until the topping is golden brown.

Baked berry custards

Preparation time
20 minutes

Cooking time
10 minutes

Serves 4

Ingredients

450 ml / 12 ½ fl. oz / 1 ¾ cups
 whole milk
4 large egg yolks
75 g / 2 ½ oz / ⅓ cup caster
 (superfine) sugar
2 tsp cornflour (cornstarch)
1 tsp vanilla extract
175 g / 6 oz / 1 ¼ cups frozen
 mixed berries, defrosted

Method

1. Preheat the oven to 180°C (160°C fan) / 350F / gas 4.

2. Pour the milk into a saucepan and bring to simmering point.

3. Meanwhile, whisk the egg yolks with the caster sugar, cornflour and vanilla extract until thick. Gradually incorporate the hot milk, whisking all the time, then scrape the mixture back into the saucepan.

4. Stir the custard over a low heat until it thickens, then divide it between four ramekins and spoon the berries on top.

5. Transfer the ramekins to the oven and bake for 10 minutes or until golden brown and set on top.

Smart tip
Cooking the custard in the saucepan first reduces the baking time considerably.

Strawberry millefeuilles

Preparation time
13 minutes

Cooking time
17 minutes

Serves 4

Ingredients

450 g / 1 lb / 1 ½ cups
   all-butter puff pastry
3 tbsp icing (confectioners')
   sugar, plus extra to serve
225 ml / 8 fl. oz / ¾ cup
   double (heavy) cream
300 g / 10 ½ oz / 2 cups
   strawberries, hulled
   and halved
3 tbsp runny honey

Method

1. Preheat the oven to 220°C (200°C fan) / 425F / gas 7.

2. Roll out the pastry on a lightly floured surface and cut it into eight identical rectangles.

3. Transfer the pastry to a baking tray and prick all over with a fork. Bake for 15 minutes or until the pastry is very crisp.

4. Dust the pastry heavily with icing sugar, then return to the oven for 2 minutes or until the sugar has lightly caramelised. Leave to cool completely.

5. Whip the cream until it holds its shape, then spoon it into a piping bag fitted with a large star nozzle. Pipe the cream onto four of the pastry rectangles and top with strawberries before laying the remaining pastry rectangles on top.

6. Put the leftover strawberries in a liquidiser with the honey and blend until smooth. Pour the sauce into a jug and serve with the millefeuilles.

Lychee and raspberry soup with marshmallow skewers

Preparation time
15 minutes

Cooking time
4 minutes

Serves 6

Ingredients

400 g / 14 oz / 2 ⅔ cups
   canned lychees, chilled
225 g / 8 oz / 1 ½ cups
   raspberries
icing (confectioners') sugar
   to taste
150 g / 5 ½ oz / 2 ½ cups
   marshmallows

Method

1. Preheat the grill to its highest setting.
2. Put the lychees and their juice in a food processor with the raspberries and blend until smooth. Taste the soup and add a little icing sugar if you would like it to be sweeter.
3. Thread the marshmallows onto wooden skewers, then toast under the grill until golden brown.
4. Pour the soup into six bowls and top each one with a marshmallow skewer.

Smart tip
Canned lychees can
be found in oriental
shops and many
supermarkets.

Index

Rice noodles
Pad Thai, *74*

Rocket (arugula)
Baked cauliflower steaks, *124*
Mixed finger rolls, *69*
Potato and rocket rosti, *31*

Rum
Mango and cardamom cheesecake pots, *197*

Salmon
Salmon and cod fishcakes, *110*
Salmon tacos with mango salsa, *131*
Salmon with Chinese cabbage and soy, *119*

Salmon, smoked
Potato waffles with smoked salmon, *23*
Scrambled egg with smoked salmon and dill, *15*
Smoked salmon and sun-dried tomato pasta, *102*
Smoked salmon pasta salad, *98*

Sausages
Chinese Sausage, brocoli and noodle stir-fry, *77*
Full English breakfast, *32*
Sesame meatball pasta, *152*

Sea bass
Steamed sea bass with lemon and lime leaves, *135*

Sesame oil
Rice noodle and green vegetable salad, *82*
Red pepper and sesame noodles, *90*
Salmon with Chinese cabbage and soy, *119*
Stir-fried duck with mangetout and sesame, *168*

Sesame seeds
Lunchbox ratatouille with chicken skewers, *61*
Red pepper and sesame noodles, *90*
Sesame meatball pasta, *152*
Stir-fried duck with mangetout and sesame, *168*

Scallops
Scallop brochettes, *156*

Shallots
Chicory, blue cheese and walnut salad, *65*
Lentil and smoked haddock salad, *160*
Potato and rocket rosti, *31*
Tabbouleh with hummus and pitta bread, *58*

Soy sauce
Chinese sausage, broccoli and noodle stir-fry, *77*
Pad Thai, *74*
Red pepper and sesame noodles, *90*
Salmon with Chinese cabbage and soy, *119*
Stir-fried duck with mangetout and sesame, *168*

Spinach
Poached egg with spinach and bacon, *24*
Smoked salmon pasta salad, *98*

Sponge fingers
Tiramisu, *206*

Squid
Chilli squid skewers with aioli, *97*

Strawberries
Baked berry custards, *214*
Fruit and turkey ham croissants, *19*
Fromage frais with strawberries and grapefruit, *35*
Speedy summer fruit gratin, *185*
Strawberry and mint tartare, *210*
Strawberry and rhubarb muesli crumbles, *182*
Strawberry millefeuilles, *217*
Strawberry verrines, *201*
White chocolate refrigerator cakes, *177*

Sugar snap peas
Rack of lamb with peas and Madeira gravy, *116*

Sweetcorn
Speedy chorizo, potato and sweetcorn stew, *155*

Taco shells
Salmon tacos with mango salsa, *131*

Tahini paste
Tabbouleh with hummus and pitta bread, *58*

Tartare sauce
Crispy fish burgers, *101*

Tomatoes
Chicken burgers with tomato and cucumber salad, *144*
Cod with tomato spaghetti, *123*
Farfalle with tomatoes, mushrooms and bacon, *139*
Full English breakfast, *32*
Goats' cheese and cherry tomato puffs, *54*
Greek salad, *62*
Jacket potatoes with tomatoes and feta, *85*
Minestrone with gnocchi, *105*
Rib-eye steak with tomatoes, *132*
Sesame meatball pasta, *152*
Smoked salmon pasta salad, *98*
Spaghetti with courgette and cherry tomatoes, *94*
Tabbouleh with hummus and pitta bread, *58*
Tagliatelle with tomatoes and olives, *81*

Tomatoes, sun-blush
Speedy summer fruit gratin, *185*

Tomatoes, sun-dried
Poached egg with spinach and bacon, *24*

Smoked salmon and sun-dried tomato pasta, *102*

Tomato passata
Chicken jalfrezi, *159*
Speedy chorizo, potato and sweetcorn stew, *155*

Turkey ham
Fruit and turkey ham croissants, *19*

Vanilla
Baked berry custards, *214*
Blackcurrant verrines, *174*
Mango and cardamom cheesecake pots, *197*
Pineapple and vanilla syrup cakes, *178*
Speedy summer fruit gratin, *185*

Veal
Breaded veal with lemon and thyme, *140*
Veal burgers, *148*
Veal, cheese and rosemary skewers, *163*

Vinegar, balsamic
Strawberry and mint tartare, *210*

Vinegar, red wine
Chicken burgers with tomato and cucumber salad, *144*

Vinegar, rice wine
Rice noodle and green vegetable salad, *82*

Vinegar, white wine
Chicory, blue cheese and walnut salad, *65*
Ham and dill pickle salad, *86*

Walnuts
Chicory, blue cheese and walnut salad, *65*
Ricotta with plums and walnuts, *39*

Watercress
Avocado and watercress on granary bread, *36*
Lamb, clementine and pomegranate salad, *106*

Wine, white
Mussels with white wine and parsley, *167*

Yoghurt, natural
Blackberry smoothie, *28*